Look Beyond the LABEL

Teens Write About Busting Stereotypes

By Youth Communication

Edited by Virginia Vitzthum

True Stories by Teens

Look Beyond the LABEL

EXECUTIVE EDITORS
Keith Hefner and Laura Longhine

CONTRIBUTING EDITORS
Philip Kay, Andrea Estepa, Tamar Rothenberg, Al Desetta, Katia Hetter, Clarence Hayes, Kendra Hurley, Nora McCarthy, Allyson G. Reid, and Hope Vanderberg

LAYOUT & DESIGN
Efrain Reyes, Jr. and Jeff Faerber

COVER ART
Photo by Minh Carrico

Copyright © 2009 by Youth Communication®

All rights reserved under International and Pan-American Copyright Conventions. Unless otherwise noted, no part of this book may be reproduced, stored in a retrieval system, or transmitted in any form or by any means, electronic, mechanical, photocopying, recording, or otherwise, without express written permission of the publisher, except for brief quotations or critical reviews.

For reprint information, please contact Youth Communication.

ISBN 978-1-935552-24-6

Second, Expanded Edition

Printed in the United States of America

Youth Communication®
New York, New York
www.youthcomm.org

Catalog Item #YD05-1

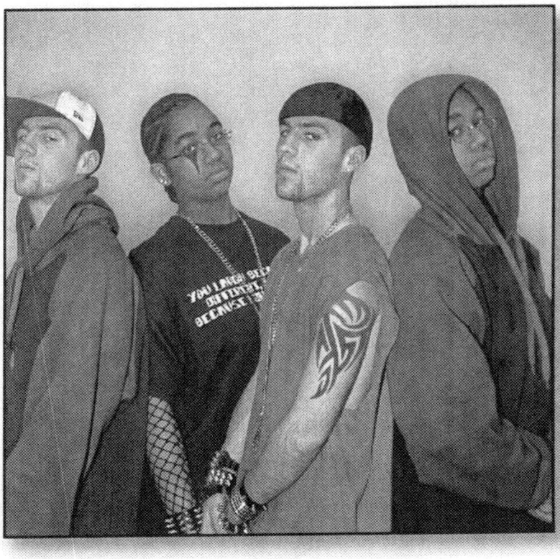

Table of Contents

Group Home Child
Keniel Simpson 15
> *Keniel is ashamed about being in foster care. But after revealing his situation to a teacher, he begins to shed his negative self-image.*

Princess Oreo Speaks Out
Dwan "Telly" Carter 21
> *Dwan is teased for "acting white"—even by family members. She wishes people would be more open-minded.*

Out, Without a Doubt
Xavier Reyes 26
> *Xavier is prejudiced against homosexuals and therefore terrified when he finds himself attracted to men. Eventually, an openly gay roomate gives him the courage to be true to himself.*

A Different Kind of Friend
LaToya Souvenir 34
> *When Latoya, who is black, becomes friends with a Puerto Rican girl, she must confront her attitudes toward people who are "different."*

Contents

Stop Following Me; I'm Not Stealing
Stephanie Hinkson 39
> Stephanie resents being scrutinized in stores because she's young, black, and stereotyped as a shoplifter.

I'm Not Who You Expect Me to Be
Jordan Yue 44
> Jordan, a Chinese-American teen, feels pigeon-holed by the "model minority" stereotype, which says that he should work hard, get good grades, and never cause any trouble.

How I Overcame a Mugging—And Prejudice
Kenneth Schlapp 51
> After getting mugged by a group of Hispanic teens, Kenneth begins to hate and fear all Hispanics. Love makes him reconsider.

Learning to Care
Sheela Pai 54
> As a new hospital intern, Sheela is afraid she won't connect with the elderly patients. But she eventually reaches out to them, breaks their isolation, and benefits as much as they do.

My Secret Love
Anonymous 61
> The writer is a tough-talking Bronx cat who sports cornrows and Timberlands. All the more reason to keep his passion for musicals a secret.

Getting Ghetto
Fred Wagenhauser 66
> First as a white boy in a black neighborhood, and then in foster care, Fred believes he has to "act ghetto" to fit in.

Dream Girl
Rance Scully 70
> Rance makes some negative assumptions about the beautiful girl he sees hanging out with the neighborhood players. But when he finally talks to her, he sees that he's misjudged her.

Rappin With the 5-0
Allen Francis 75
> A visit to a police precinct challenges Allen's stereotypes about cops.

Forbidden Territory: At Home in the Projects
Fabiola Duvalsaint 79
> Fabiola has always feared "the projects." But when she visits one, it's not what she expects.

No, I Don't Have a Pet Lion
Aissata Kebe 83
> Aissata, an immigrant from Senegal, is stunned by her classmates' ignorance about Africa and assumption about Africans.

7

He's Black, I'm Asian
Priscilla Chan 88
> A black teen helps Priscilla, who's Asian, recognize her own stereotypes and to get beyond them.

She's Cool, She's Funny, She's Gay
Sandra Leon 93
> Sandra's friends have lots of stereotypes about lesbians—but Sandra's gay sister proves them wrong.

A Classmate in a Wheelchair
Esther Rajavelu 96
> A disabled classmate causes Esther to confront her prejudices.

Why No One Knows I'm a Foster Child
Shaniqua Sockwell 99
> None of Shaniqua's friends know she's in foster care because she's afraid of being judged and teased.

The Lowdown on Aisle Seven
Tony Cedor 103
> While working at a New York supermarket, Tony is told to follow black customers around the store, even though most of the shoplifters are white.

Unwelcome in the Hood
George Yi 105
> When George, who is Chinese, moves to the Bronx, he is frequently taunted by black kids. But after a black youth befriends and defends him, George moves beyond his stereotypes.

Long-Distance Patriot
Miranda Neubauer 110
> As a U.S. citizen living in Germany, Miranda feels torn. She agrees with the widespread anger over American policies, but also wants to defend her country against simplistic stereotypes.

The Identity Experiment
Lily Mai 115
> Lily tries dressing in different styles—goth, girly, hip-hop, and her own normal look—to see how people react.

Coloring Outside the Lines
Desiree Bailey 122
> When she enters 7th grade as the only black student in her class, Desiree is thrown into confusion about her racial identity.

FICTION SPECIAL: Lost and Found
Anne Schraff 129

Using the Book

Teens: How to Get More Out of This Book....................138

How to Use This Book in Staff Training......................139

Teachers & Staff: How to Use This Book in Groups.........140

Credits... 142

About Youth Communication 143

About the Editors... 146

More Helpful Books from Youth Communication 148

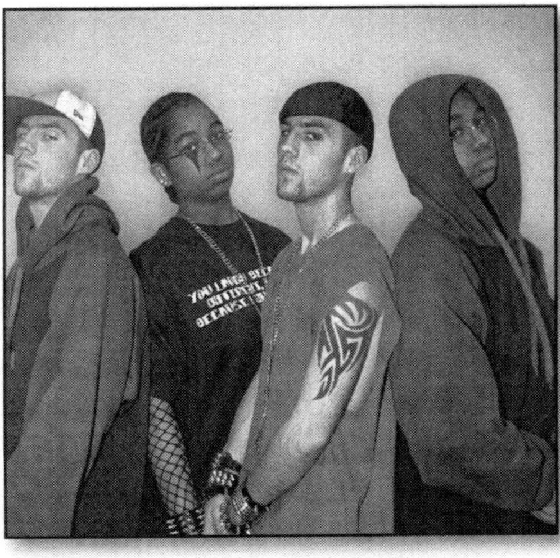

Introduction

When we stereotype people, we lose our ability to see them. Once we decide we already know who someone is because they're black or white or Chinese or gay or in foster care, we don't bother to find out what they're really like.

Several writers in this book express their frustration at being labeled and boxed in by others. Dwan Carter argues for her right to like science fiction books and pop music, even though she's black. Stephanie Hinkson has to deal with store clerks who asume that, as a black teen, she's there to steal. Because he's Chinese, everyone expects Jordan Yue to be studious, quiet, and good at math. And Aissata Kebe cannot believe the things Americans assume about life in Africa.

Other writers confront their own prejudice and explain how they came to believe myths and labels. Sometimes it's ignorance; sometimes it's the influence of their parents or their neighborhoods. LaToya Souvenir writes, "I assumed Puerto Rican girls were all rice-and-beans-eating, 'mira, mira'-yelling girls who went around cleaning up after their men all day." When she becomes friends with Lisa, who's Puerto Rican, LaToya realizes these prejudices are shared by her family and friends.

When Esther Rajavelu first noticed her discomfort around a classmate in a wheelchair, she would just avoid and ignore him. But then, she writes, "I started to deal with that 'weird' feeling I get around disabled people. I tried to be very honest about my feelings and stereotypes, and I asked a lot of questions. I think it paid off."

After Kenneth Schlapp, who's white, is mugged by a group of Hispanic boys, he thinks, "Whenever I saw a Hispanic person I felt like I either wanted to kill the person or just run away because I was afraid." But then a Hispanic girl comes to work at his ice cream store, and she surprises him. "I shouldn't have been resentful toward Hispanics," he concludes. "My resentment should have been focused on the people who committed the crime." Writers in this book also overcome assumptions about cops, people with AIDS, and even pretty girls.

Stereotypes about our own group can creep into our minds, where they cause confusion and self-hatred. "I couldn't tell her I lived in foster care, that I was a 'group home child,'" writes Keniel Simpson. "If I did, I thought she would assume that I was a delinquent. A waste of her time. A nobody."

Desiree Bailey writes, "When I saw black people lazing on street corners, or behaving inappropriately in music videos, I shook my head with disgust. I thought back to all the past struggles and achievements of black people and wondered if my generation would flush it all down the drain. Instead of looking into situations more deeply, I simply pointed my finger and criticized my people."

And Xavier Reyes writes that, when he was 12, he "always acted macho and dogged females and gays so my boys wouldn't think that I was a 'faggot.'… I believed all the lies that I heard about gays, such as all gays are not real men, they're sex maniacs, and they're all going to hell." Guess who came out as gay a few years later?

Stereotypes exist because relying on assumptions can seem easier than actually getting to know another human being. But the writers in this book show readers how rewarding it can be to do the hard work of opening your mind.

In the following stories, names have been changed: *He's Black, I'm Asian, Unwelcome in the Hood,* and *Coloring Outside the Lines.*

Group Home Child

By Keniel Simpson

I was nervous as I took a seat in the chair next to my teacher, Mrs. B. I knew she was going to ask me why I'd been missing her classes, whether my parents were aware of the fact that I had been cutting, and who I lived with. I decided that if she asked any of these questions, I was going to look her dead in the eyes and lie. I would tell her that I lived with my aunt and that I had to babysit in the afternoons. I couldn't tell her I lived in foster care, that I was a "group home child."

If I did, I thought she would assume that I was a delinquent. A waste of her time. A nobody, just because of where I lived.

I had been living in a group home for seven months. My mother had placed me there. I was ashamed of being in a group home. I was ashamed that someone else's mother took care of me, so I hid that part of my life away from my friends and teachers at school.

I couldn't look in their faces and say to them, "My mother and father abandoned me. They gave me away, turned their backs on me in my time of deepest pain and suffering."

I envied them for having a nice home to return to each day, being able to bring their friends by, for being able to say the words "Mom" and "Dad".

> **I couldn't look my friends and teachers in the face and say, "My mother and father abandoned me."**

I became reclusive. I wouldn't speak to anyone at school. I was worried that if I did, I would utter something about being in a group home. I was becoming lonely, bored, and tired too easily. I wanted a friend. I wanted that big smile on my face, too, the one the kids in school have when they are around each other.

I tried to be friends with some of the other kids in the group home. Maybe there was a person who wanted someone to talk to, someone to listen to them, someone to laugh with them, someone to just "chill out" with. But I never found that person. The boys in the house were too busy smoking cigarettes, playing video games, and talking on the phone with girls to even acknowledge me.

I now spent my days visualizing the perfect family. If I did not have any friends, at least in my imagination I could create the family I longed for, a family who loved and cared for me. I started daydreaming all day. Soon I couldn't concentrate on anything else—not on school, not on homework. I even started thinking, "Why bother going to school?"

If my mom thought that I was so bad that she'd give me, her only son, away to strangers, why should I care about tomorrow? It was just too hard.

I began leaving school early and confining myself to my room. The group home staff didn't question my early presence at home, so I didn't give them any information. Alone in my room I didn't have to watch the joy and laughter of others. I could just close the door and dream, dream of the family I longed for.

I kept telling myself that I was a nobody. Nobody. This word became cemented into my brain and became a part of my everyday vocabulary. I started believing in the word. That's what I was—a "nobody," a "group home child."

The nights became longer as I lay in my room. I felt like a bird that was caged.

"A group home. No friends. Strange people. Loneliness." These were the thoughts that crept into my bed and slept with me nightly. I wanted to escape these thoughts but I couldn't. I was only 15. I needed my mother. I needed her badly.

Slowly, all the love I had for my mother started dying like leaves falling from a tree on a wintry day. As I started to realize that she really wasn't coming back for me, that love was replaced with anger.

I once dreamed that I came home from school to my real home and my mother wasn't there. I yelled her name aloud, but no one answered. I ran to her room, then to the bathroom, then to the kitchen. Still she wasn't there. The room suddenly became dark. I began screaming, "Mom! Mom!" No one answered. My body quivered, the room was warm, I felt cold. My stomach ached. I couldn't think, my eyes began to close.

I tried calling my mother's name again, but like the volume being turned down on a radio, my voice lost its power. Then suddenly, like a painting, she appeared. She held me and we both cried. I told her never, never, to leave me again. She hugged me, kissed my forehead, and said, "I won't leave you again, I'm sorry. I'm real sorry, son."

That was the mother I wanted, the one I yearned for, but it wasn't the mother I had.

Days lapsed into weeks, which turned into months. One afternoon, my history teacher Mrs. B., who was also an assistant principal, called me into her office.

"You haven't been coming to my class and you leave school after 12 o'clock, when you have three more classes. What's the problem?" she asked.

I looked in her eyes. Those big brown eyes of hers looked sincere, caring. I opened my mouth, trying to lie, but I couldn't.

"I live in a group home." The words escaped from my mouth. I looked at her. No sudden reaction. No look of surprise. She simply mumbled, "Go on."

Suddenly, there was so much I wanted to say. So much that needed to be said. I wanted to talk about the loneliness that crept into my bed and slept with me during the nights, the absence of friends in my life, the depression I was going through, all the humiliation I felt. There were just so much that I needed to say. So much I did say.

I cried in her office. I even screamed. The feelings I had held in for so long were being released. I had been a caged bird for years. Then, like magic, the cage had disappeared. I felt free to speak, to cry, to scream, to just be me.

As I finished telling her everything I became quiet, waiting for her comment, encouragement, or insult.

"You are not a 'group home child,'" she said. "Please stop saying that. You are not alone. There's a counseling session in the leadership room every Wednesday. There are kids from group homes, foster homes, and shelters participating in the program. Stop feeling sorry for yourself. Be a part of the program. You'll meet people, have friends, feel better. And, Keniel, thank you, thanks a lot for being honest with me. I know that it was hard."

I was so happy. She had listened to me. She did not show pity because I was living in a group home. Instead, she told me how to obtain help. She told me that speaking with others is a way to deal with my problems. Her words made sense. She believed in me.

I joined the support group and began attending classes regularly. I tried hard not to feel like the nobody I had believed I was. It was difficult, but with a stop by Mrs. B's office in the afternoon, and a "B" on my history exam after a month of studying, the light became brighter for me. I knew I had a future to look forward to.

I stopped hiding the fact that I lived in a group home. Whose business was it to judge, anyway? My main concern now was to attend school as much as possible and to start socializing more, to come out of the dark and be open with others.

The program Mrs. B recommended turned out to be fun. I interacted with the other students. I also came to realize that I had many hidden talents. I am able to listen attentively to my peers, give advice, and be a genuine friend.

Meeting new people, talking about my problems, and having a support group felt so good that many nights I was able to go to bed without crying. Bit by bit, day by day, my life was now being controlled by me. I began feeling something different sneaking into my body, a sense of openness. I didn't want to contain my feelings anymore. I wanted to talk about everything—good and bad. I slowly began talking to staff in the group home. I went outside just to say hello to people.

I stopped hiding the fact that I lived in a group home. Whose business was it to judge, anyway?

I was washing from my mind the negative feelings I had about myself.

After successfully completing three years of high school, winning many awards, and being inducted into the National Honor Society, my goal is to graduate from high school and start college. I know that this dream to start college, to better my life, to let go of the past, and to forgive those who did wrong to me is possible because I want it to be.

After talking to Mrs. B, after receiving my first "B," after joining the support group, after taking control of my own life, after

Look Beyond the Label

all of this, and with much effort, motivation, and sacrifice, I've made myself a success—a person who believes in the future, who looks forward to the future, a person who wants to advance to even greater heights.

Keniel was 19 when he wrote this story. He went on to graduate from college with a degree in English Literature.

Princess Oreo Speaks Out

By Dwan "Telly" Carter

"You're just weird."

"If I wasn't looking at chu, I'd have thought you was white."

"Say that again, you said that mad white."

I often get comments like that from classmates, friends, and even my family. Sometimes I laugh back, but the comments also hurt my feelings. I know they don't mean anything by it, but I don't really like that they think I'm so strange.

I'm a dark-skinned female, a descendent of Africans. I grew up in a black family in a largely black neighborhood, and I'm conscious of the disadvantages that have plagued African-Americans for generations. So what's the deal?

It seems that, for a lot of people around me, being black is an attitude and a set of tastes. According to my peers, if you're black, you listen to hip-hop, r&b, and reggae. The ability to dance is a given. You eat Caribbean foods and Southern-style cooking, and if you're female, you know about head wraps and weaves.

Anything beyond that and it's like you're from another planet, or at least that's how I feel. I do a lot of things that people around me don't associate with being black. My friends laugh at me because I'd rather listen to Limp Bizkit than Jay-Z. They love to tease me about watching TV dramas with mostly white characters, like *Dawson's Creek* and *Felicity*.

It doesn't seem to matter that I watch *Moesha* and *The Parkers* too. Because of my tastes and the way I talk (I use big vocabulary words), people jokingly call me "Oreo": black on the outside, white on the inside.

But to me, being African-American means my skin color shows a history of enslavement and discrimination. Knowing my history and understanding where I come from is very important to me. It's what keeps me grounded and focused on taking advantage of the opportunities that African-Americans fought for.

What bothers me about being called "white"—besides the fact that I'm not—is that it seems I must be lacking something.

My dad instilled that knowledge and pride in me. As African-Americans, he says, we should be in debt to those who risked their lives to give us the opportunities we have, particularly education. His understanding of being black has a lot to do with our history and our future.

For my peers, being black has more to do with fitting into the culture right here and now. But when I try to be down with the slang and fit in, half the time I end up sounding like a fool.

"A-ight peace yo."

"You's a Doga man."

"Peace out boo-boo."

It just doesn't come out right. The words get all jumbled and tumble out wrong, and my friends look at me as if I've spoken to them in another language. All my efforts end in giggles (I'm laughing at myself right now) or in gut-busting laughter with tears streaming down my friends' faces.

My friends tease me even worse when I try to show them that I can dance to reggae, calypso, and hip-hop. It just doesn't work well. I'd never get invited to *Soul Train,* more like Soul-less Train.

It's not just friends who paint me "white." One time, my sister and I were reciting some lyrics from "You're All I Need," by Method Man featuring Mary J. Blige. My sister was reciting the rap lyrics and I was singing the hook. I was trying to be just like Mary—the bounce in her movements, the way she moved her neck, her hand motions, everything.

I was so into the song, I forgot my sister was in the room with me. I thought I was doing well until my sister's hard laughter broke my concentration. She was doubled over with tears streaming out of her eyes. She was laughing so hard she couldn't talk, and her hand was motioning for me to stop.

Then through bits of dying laughter she said, "Stop… stop trying to act ghetto, girl, you making my sides hurt." She said I looked like a duck having seizures.

Maybe I didn't move right? Since I'm African-American, I should have some rhythm, huh? And I should be able to mimic Mary? I didn't let it show, but it hurt that even my own sister didn't see me as black enough.

What bothers me about being called "white"—besides the fact that I'm not—is that it seems I must be lacking something and I'm not sure what it is.

My friend told me once, "Maybe one day you'll wake up and become Dawnesha." At the time, I was a geeky freshman in high school, insecure about who I was. I wondered if I could transform myself into someone my peers would recognize as a true black girl.

I'd have loved to put on those big hoop earrings I saw my friends wearing. I'd be wearing snake-patterned denim outfits, popping my gum, and showing off a nameplate that said

"Dawnesha." My hair would be dyed, fried, and laid to the side. And I'd rank on somebody with those fluid motions of the neck and hand that make the "African-American girl" infamous.

Sigh. I would've loved it. I just wanted to fit in. Then reality knocked some sense into me. I didn't have enough attitude to pull that off. And it just wasn't me.

Besides, Dawnesha would be as much of a stereotype as the MADtv character Bunifa. Played by Debra Wilson, Bunifa has a fierce attitude, big mouth, and snaps on anyone. Her clothes are tight, she always has her hair done and she gives her homegirl a "shout out" no matter where she is.

> **It's one thing to fit in, but my trying to be "Dawnesha" would've been like acting out a stereotyped role.**

While Debra Wilson is funny, and Bunifa does ring true in some ways, the character makes me a little angry. She's ignorant about the things around her and she always starts arguments for no reason. That's not someone I'd want to be like. It's one thing to fit in, but my trying to be Dawnesha would've been like acting out a stereotyped role.

Now, as I reach my final semester of my senior year, I'm more aware of myself, who I am, and who I want to be: me. Even saying "Dawnesha" makes me feel weird. That's not who I am. Dwan is my name and I'm comfortable with that. Being different makes me unique. I even gave myself a nickname, "Princess Oreo" (though my dad hates it).

I'm getting used to people staring at me when they hear me blasting rock music. I think it makes them feel uncomfortable because they're not used to an African-American girl bobbing her head along to rock and roll music.

"Hey," I want to tell them, "music is music." Besides, rock music was developed by black artists like Little Richard and Chuck Berry well before acts like the Beatles came along.

And there's a thin line between musical categories nowadays, and a lot of overlap in musical audiences. Plenty of white kids listen to hip-hop. And I know I'm not the only person of color who knows the lyrics to 'N Sync's "Bye, Bye, Bye."

My reading tastes are diverse, too. I like to read books by white authors, such as Isaac Asimov and Tami Hoag, as well as those by black authors, like Octavia Butler, Toni Morrison, and Malcolm X. Maybe it's because I read a lot that I talk the way I do.

It's not that I'm purposely acting white—it's not even a thought that crosses my mind. I just like what I like, and I don't know why other people can't be more open-minded.

Even though my dad emphasizes the heritage aspect of being African-American, he's not above making the same cultural assumptions as my friends. One evening, as my family and I were sitting around the dinner table, I turned on the radio and started dancing to the song "Pinch Me" by a Canadian band called Barenaked Ladies. Everyone stopped eating and gawked at me (I thought they'd be used to me by now), trying to hold back laughter.

But even when the laughter came, I kept on dancing. My dad said, "It's too late for you, girl." I knew he meant I was hopelessly white. I smiled and started to do my lame air guitar. I didn't care what they thought about me. I was happy. And that was my song.

Dwan was 18 when she wrote this story. She went on to graduate from Spelman College.

Out, Without a Doubt

By Xavier Reyes

Growing up, I always believed negative stereotypes about gays and lesbians. These stereotypes put down homosexuals and gave me an excuse to not educate myself about them. But when I got older, I learned that the only person I was dogging was myself.

When I was 12, I always acted macho and dogged females and gays so my boys wouldn't think that I was a "faggot." We always joked around about "dropping the soap" and never exchanged anything more than just a handshake. I always thought that if two guys exchanged something more than that, something was wrong.

I was extremely homophobic. I believed all the lies that I heard about gays, like that gays are not real men, they're sex maniacs, and they're all going to hell. Anytime my friends and I saw a gay person, we would make fun of him by walking "feminine."

But when I was 13, my feelings about sex began to change. For example, I once found myself looking at another guy and saying, "Damn, he's cute." When this happened, I tried telling myself that it was wrong. I ignored my feelings and they went away. Or at least I thought they did.

When I was 14, the feelings came back stronger. I thought that it was just a phase, so I continued dating girls and putting down gays. But at the same time I was scoping out other men. I still believed that there was no way in hell that I could be gay. After all, I didn't act like it.

It wasn't until I moved into Green Chimneys (a group home in New York City) that I had my eyes opened. I was now 15 and still homophobic. When I first moved in I knew there were gays there, but never expected to have one as my roommate. Because I had allowed myself to fall for myths about gays, I was extremely insecure about having a gay roommate.

I wouldn't change my clothes in front of Mike, I began to sleep in more than just my boxers, and I never walked around in just a towel. I was scared that Mike might try to hit on me or give me a surprise "wake up call" in the middle of the night and make me less of a man.

This insecurity didn't last too long because I began to get to know Mike for who he was, not what he was. I found out that we liked the same music and loved going clubbing. I didn't feel like I had to prove something in order to get his respect. But when Mike asked me if I was straight or gay, I lied and told him that I was straight but had a couple of gay friends.

The reality was that I was faking the funk. I knew I had feelings for guys, but I just didn't want to come out with it. I was afraid of being put down because of it. I didn't want people to think that I was a sissy, but at the same time I felt miserable. I was sacrificing being happy for my reputation.

After getting to know Mike better, I felt a little more comfortable with my sexuality. I didn't have to put up a front when I was with him. I grew jealous of Mike because he didn't care what people thought of him. His motto was "You get what you give." I wanted to be like him—out and without a doubt. I didn't want to live my life in a closet.

As much as I wanted to come out and be free, I still had a hard time accepting the fact that I was gay. I couldn't picture myself sleeping with another guy. I had always believed that straight men had to act masculine, play sports, and lie about what girls they had sex with. They didn't have sex with each other. If a guy was gay, then he had to be extremely flamboyant, know how to vogue, and listen to Madonna all day.

For some reason, Mike didn't seem to fit any of the stereotypes I had. He wasn't feminine, couldn't vogue to save his life, and hated Madonna. Then it hit me. I realized that I had prejudices about gays and lesbians and, until I was able to free myself from them, I couldn't accept myself.

I felt miserable. I was sacrificing being happy for my reputation.

Mike really opened my eyes and mind. I started to understand that I didn't have to be feminine or come out of the closet voguing. After about three weeks, I decided I was ready to unlock all the locks.

I called Mike into the bedroom and told him that there was something that I had to tell him. I was a nervous wreck. I had sweaty palms, shaky knees, and a dry mouth. He saw how nervous I was and immediately closed the door and asked me what was the matter.

"Mike, I want to tell you something. Please don't tell anyone yet. OK?"

"OK," he replied with a concerned expression.

"I, I, I'm, well there's a chance that..."

"What is it?" he asked, getting more and more anxious.

"Well, I could be, you know..."

"Know what?" he asked.

"I might be..."

He looked at me with this "I know you're gay" look and asked me to finish.

"I'm, well, uhm, I'm gay."

I swear, the minute I said that, I felt so relieved. I finally felt like I had no more hidden secrets. It's strange, but it felt like I was even able to breathe a little bit easier now that I had gotten this off my chest.

First Mike laughed, then he looked at me.

"Oh, I knew that," Mike said with his usual "I know everything" tone of voice. "I was just waiting to see when you were going to come out."

Mike was the first person I told I was gay. He promised not to tell anybody else. Many of the gay residents swore that I was down, but even they were skeptical.

After Mike, I didn't tell anybody else for a couple of days. I was still trying to accept who I was. Just thinking about having a boyfriend or lover made me shake my head in disbelief because I was going against everything that I thought I had believed in.

About a week later, I came out to a couple of gay residents. I always received replies like "You're gay? No way!," "It's about time," and "You need to get a man." Because my gay friends were supporting me, I decided to take my chances and tell a straight female friend.

"You're what?" Mary asked in disbelief.

"I'm gay," I repeated.

"Boy, you need to stop playing."

"I ain't playing. I'm dead up," I replied.

She looked at me and said, "You ain't one of 'em 'cause you don't act like it."

"Act like what?" I asked. By this time she was really pissing me off.

"You know," she said, putting her hand on her hip. "Fem."

"Just because I'm gay doesn't mean that I've got to act fem," I said.

Look Beyond the Label

"Well, in my book you do 'cause guys like you aren't gay."

I looked at her and walked away.

When I thought about it later on that night, I kept asking myself, "Why should I have to be fem just because I'm gay?" I finally made up my mind that I was going to be me. Regardless of what anybody said. No one could tell me how to act.

I began hanging out with my gay friends more often. We went to clubs, gay neighborhoods, and lots of gay house parties. I met a lot of kids who were my age and who were out of the closet. Some were extremely feminine while others were straight up ruffnecks. Either way, I grew really confident with myself.

When I came out to the staff in the group home, they couldn't believe it. One staff member even said, "A good-looking guy like yourself is gay? Boy, I hope there are some men left out there for my daughter."

It seemed like the more I told people, the more I wanted to come out.

Eventually, I made sure that the whole world knew. I didn't want to live my life in a closet. I had pride in who I was. The only person who didn't know was my adoptive mother.

My adoptive mother and I have always had a bad relationship. I ran away from home when I was 13 years old because I stole $1,200 from her and got caught. Growing up, my adoptive mother always spoke bad about gays. She used to say that they needed mental help, that it was immoral to be gay, and that it was "just a phase." To make matters worse, she is a Roman Catholic. They strongly believe that homosexuality is a sin. Believe me, I was not running to tell her any time soon that I was gay.

It was very easy for me to avoid having to come out to my adoptive mother. I hardly spoke with her and hardly saw her since I was living in foster care at Green Chimneys. But when I was 17 years old, I went AWOL from the group home and moved in with a friend of mine. My friend was also gay but he was much older than I was—19 years older to be exact.

The agency called my adoptive mother to let her know that I had left foster care to live on my own. My adoptive mother, of course, wanted to know where I was and who I was with. The agency gave her my telephone number and she called me.

"Hello," I asked, trying to shake the effects of deep sleep from my head.

"Xavier, this is your mother!" she screamed at me.

"Oh," I said holding the phone away from my ear. "Hello mom."

I sat up in bed while preparing my verbal weapons just in case there was an attack from the enemy lines.

"Do you know what the hell you're doing?" she asked, her voice higher than it was before.

"Here we go," I mumbled to myself.

"What!?" she screamed into my ear.

"Listen ma, this is my life. You can't tell me what to do anymore. I don't wanna be in foster care. I'm tired of being in a group home. I can take care of myself!" I screamed back at her, shocked that I actually yelled back for once.

"Well, who are you living with?" she asked. I could tell she was taken aback by my tone of independence.

"A friend, ma," I replied, trying to figure out where she was going with her questions.

"I don't know about you. But I find it pretty strange that a 17-year-old is living with a 36-year-old man!" she screamed at me.

"Ma! What do you want? So what if he's 36?" I replied.

"Is he doing anything to you?" she asked. By this time I was really upset with her.

"No, he's not doing anything to me," I said.

"Then why would a 36-year-old take in a 17-year-old?"

I thought about it for a second, then said, "He didn't take me in. I have to pay rent and pay bills just like anyone else would."

"Are you a homosexual?" she asked.

I almost dropped the damn phone on my foot. My adoptive mother was so blunt and straightforward. "Am I what?" I asked, trying to get out of telling her the truth.

"Are you a ho-mo-sex-u-al?" she said, sounding out the word as if I was learning it for the first time.

I paused for a minute, debating whether or not I should tell her. I was mad scared but I felt that this would prove to her that I was my own person. I knew that there was only so much thinking that I could do, so I let my mouth make the decision.

"Yes, I am a homosexual, " I said, emphasizing the word.

After I told my adoptive mother I was gay, she tried to tell me that I needed help. I, of course, pointed out that homosexuality was not a mental disorder. Then she tried telling me how society wouldn't accept me. I told her I didn't care what society accepts. After that, she tried dissing me by telling me that I'm not a real man. I told her straight up:

"Mom, the last time I checked below my belly button, everything was still intact. Who I decide to sleep with is my business, not yours. As long as I'm not sleeping with anybody you know, that part of my life has nothing to do with you."

She hung up on me.

Although my adoptive mother wasn't accepting of the fact that I was gay, I still felt relieved that I'd told her. I had no more secrets from her and she knew who I really was. I wasn't bothered by her homophobia. We didn't have a relationship before I came out, so it really didn't matter if we still didn't have one after I came out.

I moved back into Green Chimneys about a month later. It took three months for my adoptive mother to speak to me again. Although we still don't have a close relationship, she has come to accept me. She has told me that she is extremely old-fashioned and she knows that things have changed. She also has told me that there is nothing she can do to change my sexuality and that she has no choice but to accept it.

We had that talk eight months ago. Now she has taken the

easy way out: Don't ask, don't tell. Whenever I do talk to her nowadays, she doesn't ask, say, or even suggest anything about me being gay. It bothers me that she does this, but I also understand that she has accepted me for who I am.

Out of all the things that I have learned, the most important thing is that I cannot allow any kinds of stereotypes or prejudices to come between me and the rest of the world. I've learned the hard way that I should never judge a book by its cover. Ever since I've come out, I try to get to know people for who they are, not what they are.

> **I cannot allow any kinds of stereotypes or prejudices to come between me and the rest of the world.**

I'm not scared anymore to tell people I'm gay. In fact, I enjoy telling them because I don't fit into the stereotypes that people have about gays, and that really makes them stop and think twice. I never know when I might bump into someone who could be going through what I went through. The least that I can do for them is be out of the closet.

Xavier was 18 when he wrote this story. He graduated from college and now works for a major media company.

A Different Kind of Friend

By LaToya Souvenir

It was my first day at Murry Bergtraum HS in New York City. I sat down in Sequential Math and noted the teacher's thick glasses and his pocket protector overflowing with pens. "Of all the math teachers in this school, why did I have to be assigned The Nerd Man?" I said to no one in particular. I couldn't help it—this guy was prime dissing material.

I heard someone laugh. Sitting next to me was a Puerto Rican girl with curly, dark brown hair and braces. "Is this your first year in Bergtraum?" she asked when she finally stopped laughing.

"Yes," I said as rudely as I could. I had already made up my mind she and I were never going to become friends.

"Are you a freshman?"

"No." I thought that if I gave her only one-word answers she would leave me alone.

"What school did you transfer from?"

"Maxwell."

"Where's that?"

"Brownsville, Brooklyn. That's my neighborhood school," I said, rolling my eyes.

"Brownsville, that's where I live," she said.

Except for this one girl that used to live on my block, I had never seen Puerto Rican people in Brownsville before. Knowing that she lived in my neighborhood gave me a feeling of security in this strange, new school. Her name was Lisa, which surprised me. It was so un-Spanish. Didn't they all have names like Maria, Rosa, or Blanca?

After that, Lisa and I would say "hi" when we saw each other in the hallway. We would talk in class (the class was boring anyway). She was easy to talk to and we always made each other laugh. But I saw no reason for us to become more than school friends.

Her being Puerto Rican was still in the back of my mind. Other than a girl named Rosa in junior high school, I had never even met a Puerto Rican before. My elementary school, junior high, old high school, my neighborhood, even my church were all predominantly black. I rarely had the chance to interact with people of other races. I was used to being around my own people and I wasn't about to change.

I assumed that all Puerto Rican girls were like Rosa from junior high: rice-and-beans-eating, "mira, mira"-yelling girls who went around cleaning up after their men all day.

Was Lisa going to be like that? What if she wanted to hug and kiss each time we saw each other? I was not down with that.

What if she spoke Spanglish and I couldn't understand her? What was I supposed to call her—Hispanic? Latino? Puerto Rican? Would she be insulted if I picked the wrong one? I imagined that because she was of a different race, I would have to speak to her differently.

For all of sophomore year, Lisa and I remained casual acquaintances. In junior year our schedules changed and we no longer had the same math class. We hardly ever saw each other. Then one day, on my way home from school, I saw Lisa on my train.

It turned out that we only lived a few blocks apart and had never once stumbled across each other. After that discovery, we began to ride the train to and from school together.

> **I was used to being around my own people and I wasn't about to change.**

Besides going to the same school and living in the same neighborhood, it turned out that the two of us had a lot in common. We were both the oldest in our families, both have brothers, and both live in houses (not apartments) with both our parents. Recently, we discovered that both our mothers have a ridiculous rule about not allowing us to have a guy in our bedroom.

Lisa and I started hanging out together in and out of school. We would often walk to class together, or meet up afterwards. I introduced her to my friends and family, and she introduced me to hers. We even made new friends together.

But it wasn't always easy. When I told my mom about my new friend she just said, "Oh." She never said anything more but she didn't have any Puerto Rican friends and I don't think she was particularly thrilled that I did.

One time Lisa and I were walking up the street in Brownsville when my friend Mel called me over. After a couple minutes, he looked at Lisa and asked, "What's she doing over here? You wanna show her what a ghetto look like?"

"No," I said looking at him like he was stupid. "She lives over here." This wasn't the first time people had made ignorant comments about Lisa.

"Well, why I ain't never seen her before?"

"Maybe you just wasn't looking."

At first I was shocked at how prejudiced so many of my friends were, but by this point I was just tired. I was tired of them acting like she was some sort of specimen on display. She was a person just like the rest of us.

"Oh please, Toya. I woulda seen her. She is a little light for Brownsville," he said.

"Oh, shut up," I told him. I wasn't in the mood to listen to any more of his garbage. I understood where it came from, because I grew up in Brownsville too and I had a little bit of that garbage in my head also. But luckily I had started to overcome it.

"I'm gonna see you later," I said. "I have to go do some homework."

"Yeah a'ight, Toya," he said, as if he didn't believe me.

Over time, Lisa and I became inseparable. During senior year, I actually started hanging out at her house.

I really like her family. Lisa's father spends time with his children, he jokes around and plays with them, and they talk to each other. With her mother, she can talk about anything.

The entire family eats dinner together, which I think is wonderful. Every year for Christmas they choose the house of an aunt, uncle, or grandparent, and everyone spends the day there, opening presents and singing carols. Someone even dresses up as Santa Claus and passes out the gifts. I wish my family did those things.

At first, I would go over there maybe once every two weeks; now, I am over there almost every day. I often go shopping with her mother, and sometimes we go visit her mother's friends. Her father has even begun to call me his "adopted daughter." Everyone on her block knows me; it's like I live there.

Lisa and her family have destroyed my stereotype of Puerto

> *I was tired of my friends acting like Lisa was some sort of specimen on display. She was a person just like the rest of us.*

Rican people. She doesn't want a kiss every time we see each other; in fact, she never wants a kiss. She speaks as much English as I do, and like me, she speaks differently when she's at home.

Thanks to this wonderful friend and Murry Bergtraum HS, I am learning to get rid of some of the garbage that has collected in my head. At Bergtraum, with its Chinese principal and faculty and students of every conceivable race, I couldn't escape the fact that there isn't a set mold that all people of a particular group fit into. Maxwell, my old school in Brownsville, was pretty much all black so I never had to think about those things.

My problem hasn't been completely cured. I still sometimes lapse into making broad generalizations about an entire group of people just because I meet one fool who happens to live up to the stereotype. But I can say that I have come a long way.

Despite the narrow-minded attitudes I inherited from my parents, my neighborhood, and society at large, I'm proud to say that I actually made friends with a Puerto Rican, someone I once believed was too different for that ever to be possible.

It's been four years since that day in math class and Lisa still listens to my problems no matter how silly they may seem, and no matter how late I may call. When I need someone to pour my heart out to, to solve my problems, or to tell me how rude I'm acting, Lisa is always there. Although it took me some time to realize it, she is my true friend.

LaToya was 18 when she wrote this story. She graduated from college and has worked for several nonprofit organizations.

Stop Following Me; I'm Not Stealing

By Stephanie Hinkson

"Excuse me, miss, do you need help?"

"No, thank you. I do not."

That's how it often starts. She asks me if I need help and pretends to fix something. I move, she moves. I stop, she stops. I turn around, she watches. You should be getting the pattern by now.

I am in a store shopping. I am African-American and young, and so she, the store employee, thinks I'm going to steal. What's funny is that the employees are of all races. Yes, the black and Hispanic ones are on my back also.

Most of the time, it takes them less than two minutes after I walk into the store to get within a few feet of me. Their faulty radar turns their eyes laser-beam red and they fly over to me in no time, pretending to fix the shirts on the rack or the pants on the shelf behind me. The point when it really hits me that they're watching me like a surveillance camera is when I'm focused on the clothes I'm about to buy and realize they haven't moved.

This is when I get angry. This is the 21st century and I feel like people still can't get past the color of my skin. Yes, I want to buy something from your store. I am not going to steal and I feel angry that anyone would suspect me of doing so.

I don't see myself as a target for suspicion. I'm quiet and I dress nicely. I usually wear high heels and dressy shirts. I don't like looking like everyone else my age. I believe the impression you make is important and I carry myself maturely.

> **Store employees fly over to me in no time, pretending to fix the shirts on the rack or the pants on the shelf behind me.**

I wouldn't shoplift because my mother taught me better than that. I'm a Christian and I believe that stealing is wrong. Plus, it's a crime and I'd never do anything to jeopardize my future. So if someone assumes differently, I feel offended. They don't understand who I am.

I first try to ignore the "red eye" so I can keep my cool and continue looking at the clothes. But if she's still right behind me, I ask, "Is there a problem?"

"Problem? There's no problem," is the usual reply.

"Well, I think there is because you have been following me since I came into the store and I didn't ask for any help, so can you please excuse me?" I've said this more times than I can remember.

Sometimes they'll apologize and try to appear sorry. Other times they glare at me like they want to take it outside. Whenever that happens I let them know, "If there is a problem I can always go speak to your manager." That's when they back off.

One day I went shopping with my friend Tiffany, who's African-American also, at Kings Plaza mall in Brooklyn, New York. We went into a shoe store, where there were other customers shopping. As we made our way up one aisle, there was the red eye.

We went down the aisle—so did the red eye. By the next aisle I knew what was going to happen. "Tiffy, let's leave, 'cause we are being followed," I told my friend.

"Yeah, for real," Tiffany replied.

We left the store, but that company has a clothing section in a different part of the mall, and after we stopped somewhere else, that's where we went. Believe it or not, we saw the same red eye in that store. When we saw her, Tiffany and I looked at each other and started laughing. She didn't follow us in this store though. I think she'd heard us in the previous store and had gotten the gist of things.

Some people ask if being suspected of shoplifting is a race issue or an age issue for me, and I think it's both. When I asked my mother and a couple of other adults of color if they feel like they get followed in stores, their answer was, "Hardly ever." Yes, it might happen once or twice, but not the way it happens to me.

To be fair, it's true that more teenagers are caught shoplifting than any other age group. And I know teens who steal. Sometimes teenagers shoplift to impress their friends, or to fit in by doing whatever their friends are doing. Some teenagers steal because they have no money and they don't want to be teased for not having the newest name-brand clothes. I've also seen people selling their shoplifted goods on the street to make money.

But I don't think I'm followed just because I'm young.

Anna, a classmate of mine who's white, said she's seldom been followed in stores. And she told me about an incident she saw in a jewelry store. "I saw two female friends together," Anna said. One was black and one was white. "As I was looking at them," Anna said, "the white girl took something."

One of the store clerks suspected something and walked up to the two of them, but approached the black girl, and the white girl walked out of the store. "The true culprit got off," Anna said. The friends were both young, but the black girl got singled out.

Anna's story upset me but it didn't surprise me. There have been many times when I've been in a store and white people weren't followed but I was.

And many adults of color report discrimination in stores, too. In a Gallup poll, almost a third of the black adults surveyed said that in the previous month, they'd been treated unfairly in a store because they were black.

I understand that shoplifting is a problem. Stores lose out when people steal. An annual survey of stores estimates that nationwide there are about a million shoplifting incidents every day, totaling a loss of around $10 billion a year.

But store management's acting as if only certain races steal doesn't benefit them. In 2002, Sharon Simmons-Thomas, an African-American secretary, sued Macy's for racial profiling. She said that though innocent of shoplifting, she was detained and mistreated by Macy's security personnel because of her race.

Macy's paid to settle the case in 2004, so it didn't go to trial. In January 2005, Macy's settled another lawsuit over alleged racial profiling of black and Latino customers, brought by New York's attorney general. Macy's had to pay $600,000 in damages and change its security practices.

Sometimes I ask to speak to the manager, which usually results in the employee trying to apologize and keep it hush-hush.

Teenagers who feel like they are obvious targets for the red eye don't have to stand there and take it. I've been followed enough times that I've figured out how to deal with it.

Sometimes I ask to speak to the manager, which usually results in the employee trying to apologize and keep it hush-hush. Or I'll decide not to spend my money in that particular store, and leave. If you follow me down like a scavenger to fresh meat then I do not need to spend my money in your store.

If you're an honest person, you should not be made to feel like a criminal. And if you are a teenage shoplifter, you're making it hard on the rest of us. Shoplifting is a crime and you can go to jail for it. Think twice before you take something.

Finally, to all of you red eyes: The next time you see a young person of color in your store, keep in mind that all minorities do not steal, and neither do all teens.

Stephanie was 18 when she wrote this story.

I'm Not What You Expect Me to Be

By Jordan Yue

"You're good at math, right?"

Both Asian and non-Asian classmates have said that to me, throwing it out in casual conversation as we're walking to class.

Actually, I'm just OK at math. But it bothers me that they seem to think I'd be a math whiz just because I'm Chinese-American and there's a common idea that Chinese—and Asians in general—are good at math. I feel like people have certain assumptions about me simply because when they look at me, they see "Chinese" or "Asian."

The stereotype goes beyond math skills. Asians are called the "model minority" because we're the minority group that people say succeeds best in America; according to the stereotype, we work hard, stay quiet and don't cause trouble. An Asian student is valedictorian? No big surprise. According to the stereotype, we're both disciplined and naturally smart.

It's not like the stereotype comes from nowhere. In Chinese culture, for example, education and discipline are very important. Throughout Chinese history, scholars were the most respected people in society. Martial arts, tai chi and Confucian principles also teach discipline, so it makes sense that discipline plays an important part in the culture.

That might sound good to you, but the flip side is that we're also considered sexless (or at least the guys are), socially inept and easily picked on. And even the "good" parts of the stereotype bug me, because I feel like people look at me and automatically see someone I'm not.

Now, I'm not gonna front. In some ways I do fit this stereotype, at least the academic part. I go to Bronx Science, a competitive school that you have to take a test to get into; more than 40% of my school is Asian.

But in other ways, I feel like the stereotype isn't me, and even if I wanted to be that way and tried, I couldn't do it. I'm also mad at the reality behind the stereotype; at home, I get the kind of pressure to do well that really is common in Asian families. I feel like both outsiders and my own parents expect me to be the "model minority."

Ever since I can remember, I haven't matched people's expectations. I'm a third generation Asian-American—this means it was my great-grandparents who immigrated here—and in lots of ways I feel more American than Chinese. I don't speak Chinese. I like basketball. I listen mostly to hip-hop, reggae, blues, rock and r&b. I hate going to school. I curse like a sailor. I'm interested in the latest sneakers coming out. I'm your typical New Yorker.

Back when I was a young'un, I wasn't treated warmly by

most of the Asian kids. You see, my area of Flushing, Queens, is mostly first and second generation Koreans and some Chinese; most of the kids' parents were immigrants, and some of them were, too.

I didn't understand Chinese and I didn't speak with an accent, so they often accused me of trying to be white. Whether it was at school or in the neighborhood playing ball, they made it clear that I didn't fit in. I did have friends, who varied in race, but I was a lunchroom table-hopper, trying out different groups to see if I fit in.

At home, my parents expected me to be a good student. An 80 on a test wasn't good enough. It sometimes seemed that they wanted me to exceed some unsaid limit. For the most part this didn't bother me. I did my work in school and didn't cause too many problems. Up to 7th grade I was relatively obedient and performed well throughout the year.

> *I feel like both outsiders and my own parents expect me to be the "model minority."*

Still, my heroes were loner rebel characters like Han Solo, a leader of the Rebel Alliance in the Star Wars trilogy, and Wolverine of the X-Men. Wolverine is hotheaded, doesn't always listen to Cyclops or Professor X, and always seems pissed off and ready to fight because he was either misunderstood or treated wrongly. I looked up to these rebels, who were much more fascinating than the do-gooder, wholesome characters like Superman.

It wasn't until 8th grade that I started acting up in class. I wasn't doing as well in school, and my teachers started sending notes home to my parents. They got mad and yelled at me, so then I'd yell back. I felt that my parents were simply putting more pressure on me rather than hearing me out.

Not that I knew what exactly was bothering me; I just felt 8th grade was a waste of time. I was disruptive and made inappropriate comments in my classes and to teachers. At the time, I felt that I was funny, even if classmates were telling me to shut up.

But though part of me was having fun, part of me was also angry. I didn't want to be obedient and quiet. I was angry at my parents, who I felt were blaming me without acknowledging their own contributions to my behavior. But I was angry at myself, too, because I had done well the year before and I just couldn't see why I was doing poorly this year.

I felt that nobody understood me and worse, no one cared to try; they all had their pre-formed ideas about who I was supposed to be: a good, hardworking, quiet Asian kid. A lot of the other Asian kids around me were like that, though some had more attitude than me, going the gangster route to be tough.

The worse I felt, the angrier I got, and the more trouble I got in. I was acting out and not handing in my work, and my parents were furious over the letters they were getting about my cutting. I wasn't happy with myself, but my parents yelling at me so much didn't exactly motivate me to make the right choices.

I felt that I didn't fit in at home or at school, but I didn't know why or how to change the situation. Then I started thinking about how I fit into society when, the summer after 8th grade, I picked up a book called *Eastern Standard Time*, which is about Asian culture in America.

The book brought to my attention the "model minority" stereotype and opened up a world of thought for me. The book said that the image of a studious, disciplined achiever was something that grew out of Asian values and suggested that it's both positive and negative.

At first I thought I liked the idea of the model minority stereotype, since it meant that society expected me to succeed; I wasn't feeling like anyone expected me to succeed after my miserable time in 8th grade.

Yet when I gave it more thought, I realized how bad the stereotype was. It put down other minorities by implying that none work harder than Asians. And it labeled me as something I wasn't: a focused overachiever who doesn't rock the boat.

Learning about the model minority stereotype made me realize why so many Asians I knew were stressed about grades. The book helped me think about the expectations I was resisting at school and at home; it was like people expected me to get good grades and be obedient just because I was Asian—not because I was Jordan. It made me angry at the stereotype, and a little less angry at myself.

Still, I entered high school with the same rebellious attitude I'd had through junior high. I was loud and obnoxious in my high school classes and was almost suspended for throwing a book at my freshman year global history teacher (though really I was passing it to its owner across the room—through the air).

Even though I avoided suspension, I was still doing badly in school. Finally, that spring, I was diagnosed with a mild case of attention deficit disorder (ADD). ADD is a learning problem that causes the person who has it to be easily distracted, and makes it harder for him or her to concentrate.

Finding out about my ADD made me feel like I stood out even more, especially since I was Asian. How stereotypically Asian could I be when I had to take medication just to sit quietly in class and learn? But the medication helped me focus, and I didn't feel the same impulse to blurt out wise-ass comments in class. I felt more in control, and in a way, that made me less angry.

Since I wasn't as obnoxious in class, things got better. Even though I wasn't the model minority child my parents wanted me to be—and I was still mad at them for expecting me to be that way—I wasn't feeling so bad about myself.

And in 9th grade, I found the group of people I'm most cool with and comfortable around, who happen to be mostly black and Hispanic. I do have Asian and white friends, but race isn't an issue for me in making friends; it's about personality.

Two of my best friends—Ian and Ptah, who are black—were more focused than I was about school, which was a good influence on me when I was angry over yet another failed test.

I related to them because they know how to balance doing well in school with being able to get down, chill and party on the side. I didn't have to choose between the total rebel or the total goody two-shoes. I could be a balance of both, which I think is how I naturally am.

Ptah told me once that he thinks the stereotypes Asians have to deal with aren't bad. He feels the stereotypes blacks are subjected to, like being thugs and drug dealers, are much worse. I understand his point of view, but I still don't like being boxed in by a list of assumptions that don't fit me.

The problem with any stereotype is that it gets in the way of people seeing you as an individual. Stereotypes are like an outside skin that people should learn to see past. People are deep and complex. Everyone has a story to tell, something different to say. Everyone wants recognition, and labeling people with stereotypes makes the individual disappear.

> **I didn't have to choose between the total rebel or the total goody two-shoes. I could be a balance of both.**

When people say stuff to me about Asians being good at math or Asians being quiet, I tell them my experience. Sometimes, though, I just let it slide because I don't feel like arguing.

In some ways, I feel like I've escaped the stereotype. I'm happier being myself, kicking it with people who accept me for whoever I am.

After freshman year, my parents lowered their standards for me. They accept that I'm going down my own path—which does include college, even if it's not the Ivy League as my mom was hoping. Things are calmer at home, which is a relief.

It's funny how easy it is to stereotype each other when most of us want to be seen as the individuals we are. I'm Jordan: The loud, obnoxious, college-bound Asian-American kid from Flushing, Queens, who has something to say.

Jordan was 17 when he wrote this story. He went on to college at SUNY New Paltz, majoring in public relations.

How I Overcame a Mugging—And Prejudice

By Kenneth Schlapp

It was 3 o'clock in the afternoon on a cold March day. After school, my daily ritual was to go to the deli on Suydam Street nearby to pick up the newspaper, then walk home. On this particular occasion I had an extra $20, because I was supposed to stop at the butcher shop on my way home.

I walked out of the store and through a crowd of people coming out of the high school. I was carefree--the thought of a problem arising was the furthest thing from my mind. Then, out of nowhere, someone punched me in the eye.

My first instinct was to walk away because I was suddenly aware that I was the only white person in a crowd of Hispanics. I was scared. The next thing I knew, someone grabbed me from behind and four or five people started hitting me. I thought they'd never stop. It occurred to me that if they wanted to kill me, there was nothing I could do to stop them.

They finally decided to stop hitting me, but not before taking my jacket and the $20. After they left, I noticed at least 40 people standing around watching like it was a show and not a criminal act. I got up and walked away as fast as I could. My house was only a block away. I rang the bell, and my mother answered. She saw that my mouth was bloody, my eye was bruised, my hair was disheveled, and my jacket was gone. She took one look at me and started crying.

> **I was suddenly aware that I was the only white person in a crowd of Hispanics.**

We decided I should go to the hospital to check my head for fractures. It turned out that there wasn't anything seriously wrong, but I had a three-day headache and I couldn't eat anything that was tough to chew because my jaw was in so much pain.

I lived through that, but I didn't know if I would be able to live with the knowledge that nobody cared to help me. I realize that I was in a Hispanic neighborhood and that I was the only white person in sight, but to watch someone being beaten up without a thought of helping is just inhuman.

Before this happened, I never even thought about people being of different races. I thought of everyone as the same. It didn't matter what neighborhood I walked in, I was never afraid or felt like I was above other people because they were of a different race. I had walked down Suydam Street many times before, but I never thought anything like this would occur. After I got mugged, I wouldn't even walk past the deli on my way to the subway station, much less go in.

I started negatively stereotyping all Hispanics, not just the ones who hurt me. The resentment I felt was very strong. I couldn't stand the sight of them. Whenever I saw a Hispanic person I felt like I either wanted to kill the person or just run away because I was afraid. I wouldn't even think about associating with a Hispanic person until many months later.

My opinion began to change after I met my girlfriend, who is Hispanic. We met at a Carvel store. I was the manager of the store and she was starting her first day, so it was my job to train her.

I figured she was just like all the other Hispanics: loud, a troublemaker, had an attitude against whites, and listened to hip-hop and salsa. Even though I was resentful of Hispanics, I wouldn't come right out and show it, so I was polite while training her.

I found out I was wrong, though, because I was able to get along with her really well from the start. Then one day I noticed that she was wearing a Pink Floyd button. I was surprised. I asked her if she liked rock. She told me she did.

I said to her, "I was surprised to see the Floyd button because not many Spanish people listen to rock." There were many realizations after that. I began to view Hispanics differently. I stopped avoiding people because they were Hispanic. I learned that people shouldn't be stereotyped by their race, and an entire race of people can't be judged by one incident.

I learned that an entire race of people can't be judged by one incident.

I realize now that, out of fear for themselves, most people wouldn't help someone who is being beaten up. I shouldn't have been resentful towards Hispanics. My resentment should have been focused on the people who committed the crime.

Kenneth was 17 when he wrote this story. He graduated from Hunter College and went on to become a manager and writer.

Learning to Care

By Sheela Pai

In the spring of my freshman year, I started noticing these pink fliers on bulletin boards everywhere at school. After a while I decided to actually read one. It turned out to be an announcement of a six-week summer internship in health and medical careers at Coler Memorial, a local hospital.

I had been looking for something different to do with my summer and I liked the idea of meeting doctors and following them around the hospital. I figured that taking care of patients would be OK too; the most I'd probably have to do would be to push them around in their wheelchairs or read them a book.

On my first day of work I was ready to jump into the world of medical careers. Instead, all the interns were led into a conference room and we were told that we'd undergo a week of patient care training. "What do they mean?" I thought. "How could they do this to me?"

I thought taking care of patients meant pushing their wheelchairs, feeding them, and making their beds. But I soon found out there was much more to it than that. We learned about patients' rights and were taught how important it is to listen to them and understand their situations. We were expected to talk to the patients, something that had never crossed my mind.

There were also hands-on activities that helped "sensitize" us to difficulties caused by different handicaps. In one we had to pretend we were paraplegics (people who've lost the use of their arms or legs). In another we had to pour ourselves glasses of water with blindfolds on.

The results were hilarious. By the time it was over, my shirt was soaking wet and I was nauseous because when I was going up a ramp, my wheelchair started rolling backwards very fast, out of control. I was fortunate to come out of it without a scratch.

I originally expected Coler Memorial to be a nice little hospital with freshly tiled walls and happy patients carrying get-well cards and balloons while their relatives smothered them with affection. Instead it was a dreary place. Patients with knotty, unwashed hair and thin, stained cotton hospital gowns were stationed in their wheelchairs in dimly lit hallways. Some just looked at you through glazed eyes and others screamed lewd remarks because they'd lost their inhibitions as they grew older.

To them, Coler Memorial wasn't just a hospital, it was their home. All of them, from few-month-old babies to hundred-year-old senior citizens, were there because afflictions like AIDS, multiple sclerosis, and severe mental illness prevented them from taking care of themselves. Their relatives, if they had any, couldn't handle taking care of them either.

After training, I was assigned to spend the first half of every day with patients. My first one was Ms. H. I was afraid that she'd throw a fit as soon as she saw me and say she wanted to be left alone. When I entered her room, however, she was sitting quietly in a wheelchair and watching *Family Feud*. She looked like a typical sweet granny. Her face was heavily powdered and her short white hair was neatly combed back. She seemed to notice me but was deliberately ignoring me.

Cautiously, I walked up to her and told her I'd be her "friend" for the next few weeks. (I didn't use the word "intern" because it seemed so cold and sterile.) Ms. H didn't seem to understand, and asked quickly, with a heavy Polish accent, "What are you talking about?"

Scared that she hated me, I tried to think of something we could do together. I suggested I take her to the garden since it was a beautiful summer day. She readily agreed and in a matter of moments we were outside smelling the fragrant flowers and soaking in the sunshine. She was quiet except for when she made one or two brief comments in clipped English about how funny the pigeons in the garden were.

Suddenly, she ordered me to take her upstairs. "I have to get my lunch ticket," she announced. I didn't understand what she meant. I knew the residents had their lunches delivered to their beds at 11 o'clock every day. I then realized that she was probably mixing up something from the past with the present, because she kept on talking about lunch lines, which I knew didn't exist. Calmly, I told her there was no such thing as a lunch ticket. But my reassurance did no good; she kept on insisting that I take her back to her room.

Without another word, I took Ms. H back inside. While I watched her eat lunch and watch TV, I wondered how I was going to survive the next six weeks with her, and I prayed that my other patient wouldn't be like this too.

When I went to visit my other patient, Ms. N, she was lying very quietly on her bed, watching TV. I was scared that she'd be quiet and apathetic, but I quickly discovered that Ms. N was full of life. From the moment we met we had a million things to talk about. I'd bring her magazines and sit by her bed and we'd gossip about celebrities and find faults in every model photographed.

Ms. N told me stories about her husband, her son, and her youth. The funniest ones were about accepting dares from her classmates back in nursing school and sneaking into the kitchen and getting caught by the "house mother."

Ms. N couldn't move her hands, so another intern and I would read aloud selections from the book series based on the soap opera *One Life To Live*. My friend and I would act out all the mushy, I-love-you scenes using exaggerated gestures and weepy voices just to get Ms. N to laugh.

Meanwhile, my relationship with Ms. H steadily improved. Gradually, I started prying information out of her. Her background was really interesting. She and her husband had immigrated from Europe when she was in her 20s. Once she arrived in America, she got a job designing children's clothing. I imagined Ms. H creating pastel-colored pinafores and adorable little overalls. For the first time I saw her maternal side.

Even though I knew you couldn't catch AIDS just by touching someone, I was still scared.

One day when I took Ms. H to the garden, another resident walked up to her and shyly handed her a red rose. The rest of the day I teased her about her new "boyfriend" while she giggled like a teenage girl.

Unfortunately, I struck a sore spot when I asked Ms. H about her daughter. In a faked, uncaring tone, she brushed away the question by saying her daughter was in California and was coming to visit her very soon. Later I found out from a staff member that Ms. H's daughter had abandoned her there and never really visited. I then realized how hard it must be for Ms. H to open up after being betrayed and forgotten by her own child.

In addition to spending time with our patients, the other interns and I also learned more about medicine. Every Friday afternoon, we would either listen to a doctor lecture or visit a special ward. One of the most memorable visits was to the AIDS ward.

Even though I had done a presentation on AIDS in biology class that year and knew you couldn't catch it just by touching someone, I was still filled with naive fears when I entered. I stuck my hands deep in my pockets so I wouldn't have any exposed skin.

One young man, who was in his 20s at the most, was lying in bed weakened and crippled by disease. Still he managed to ask us about our experience as interns so far. Occasionally he'd gesture weakly with his pale, bony arms. When some of us would make jokes, he'd softly chuckle and grin. It was like he had an invincible spirit.

After a while, I started to loosen up a little. My hands slipped out of my pockets and I started paying more attention to what the doctor was saying about the patients instead of scrutinizing how they looked.

When I was leaving the ward, a woman covered with lesions and wrinkles started shuffling toward us. She was wearing a tattered hospital gown and was hunched over. Though we knew from a nurse that she was in her 40s, the woman looked like she was 80 years old. "Come back and visit," she hollered after us. As much as I wanted to, I didn't know if I had enough stamina to face this kind of suffering again.

One rainy day, I was working in another ward and I was bored out of my mind. All the patients, including mine, were very sluggish and just wanted to watch TV. A couple of other interns and I were watching a nurse put lipstick on a resident in the recreation room when we all came up with an idea to perk up the day. Makeovers!

Another female intern and I went to the head nurse for beauty supplies. She gave us bundles of nail polish bottles, orangewood sticks, nail files, and lipsticks. We divided ourselves into pairs and went to visit the residents in their rooms.

I was surprised that most of them were eager to get makeovers. They giggled when I told them that I was giving them a "French beauty renewal" (not that I really know what that means). I knew I was making a difference when one lady, who would always sit silently on her bed, looked in the mirror afterwards and exclaimed with a soft smile, "Ooh, I look beautiful!"

Working at Coler Memorial gave me a chance to make a difference in a few people's lives, but more importantly it helped me grow as a person. Before my internship, I always thought I had been exposed to people from all different walks of life and had an open mind.

My greatest accomplishment was successfully reaching out to people who had isolated themselves.

I thought if I met a person with AIDS, for example, I wouldn't be the least bit afraid since I knew the facts. Instead, I found out that, like any other human being, I had fears that could only be controlled, not erased. I discovered that I still had a lot to learn about myself.

Before, when I saw a person in a wheelchair, I'd be tempted to look at her out of the corner of my eye since it seemed so unusual. Now I realize that paralysis and other handicaps are a way of life for the people who have them and should be treated like that by the rest of us.

I feel my greatest accomplishment was successfully reaching out to people who had isolated themselves. Ms. H. never said very much, but I always made a point of dropping by her room every morning and saying "hi" to her. I'd ask her if she needed help with anything and would sometimes help her arrange her drawers.

Towards the end of the program, I was disappointed that I hadn't been able to get her to really open up to me. On my last

Look Beyond the Label

day of work, I went to say goodbye to her. I expected her to just say "bye" and go about her business. Instead, she told me she appreciated all that I'd done for her and went on about what a good person I was and how she hoped the very best for me.

I left the hospital that day surprised yet content. Perhaps I had affected these patients' lives just as much as they had mine.

Sheela was 16 when she wrote this story. She went to Yale and the University of Pennsylvania Law School. She is now a lawyer in New York City.

My Secret Love

By Anonymous

I was born and raised to walk and talk tough and spit with dignity and class. I know who to watch out for on the street, like dudes who carry liquor bottles and wear too much red. (There are a lot of gang members around my way.)

The way I dress reflects my neighborhood, so most people expect my taste in music to follow the same pattern. Mean streets + the latest jeans + cornrows + Timberlands = hard-core rap 24/7.

That's partially true, because hip-hop is a major part of my life. But there's also a hidden part of me. It's not something I like to talk about, even if you paid me. If I did, people would laugh long and loud. It's not easy for me to admit this, but…

I love musicals.

Yep. *The Sound of Music, The King and I, Carousel, West Side Story*…you name it, I've seen and enjoyed it.

Look Beyond the Label

I like the emotions given off by musicals, the way the story and the songs blend together to make a single presentation filled with dancing and catchy show tunes. I like watching Mary Poppins fly around with an umbrella, singing about medicine going down nicely if you take sugar with it.

But you're not listening. You're too busy laughing at me. The way I began this story, you probably thought I had a drug problem. If I did, I would have gladly put my name on this article. No one would laugh at me if I was addicted to cocaine.

Musicals and I go way back. *The Sound of Music* was the first one I saw, back in 6th grade. My teacher rolled the TV into the room, switched the lights off, and let the show begin. I sighed and braced myself for what I thought would be the whackest class of my 11 years.

But then, when the characters started singing, it suddenly became interesting to me. Characters would be talking about something, then they would just jump into song. As I watched the film, I realized I was being introduced to a revolutionary concept—a full-length movie that conveyed emotions through music and singing.

In one of the most memorable scenes, the main character, Maria (played by Julie Andrews), comforts the kids she is taking care of. The children are scared of a raging storm, so she begins to sing about her "favorite things" to take their minds off their fear.

A few weeks after the viewing, the entire school had to do renditions of various musical numbers on stage in the auditorium. My class had to sing "Sixteen Going on Seventeen" from *The Sound of Music*. One part was sung by the girls and the other part by the fellas. We did well, and my self-confidence never faltered during the performance.

But after my performance in 6th grade, I lost interest. My attention span was really short when it came to new things. Musicals were the last thing on my mind until my senior year of high school.

My music teacher rekindled my interest. He showed flicks like *Carousel* and *West Side Story* to our class every week as examples of different kinds of music. The other kids didn't appreciate it at all, but every day I secretly hoped he'd continue showing them.

My music teacher was gay and white, so admitting that he liked musicals didn't hurt his reputation at all. I, on the other hand, wouldn't be able to take the "Oh yeah, he's gay too" stares I knew I would get if people knew my secret.

But one day, I took a chance and admitted to some friends at work that I had watched a few musicals.

"Come on, sing a show tune you know," someone said.

"Yeah, don't be shy."

"Why not?" I said after a moment's hesitation.

> **No one would laugh at me if I was addicted to cocaine, but I can't tell anyone I love musicals.**

I attempted to repeat my stellar 6th grade performance in response to the earnest requests of my co-workers. So I started singing that still familiar song in a mock soprano voice.

"I am 16, going on 17, I know that I'm naïve…fellows I meet may tell me I'm sweet, and willingly I beleeeeive…"

(OK, so for some strange reason, I only remembered the girl's part.)

Instead of applause for my attempt to bestow culture upon them, what followed was 10 minutes of uncontrollable laughter. And mocking.

Ingrates.

But really, what's so bad about liking musicals? The music is catchy and you have visuals. They're similar to the modern music video, but they differ because videos focus mainly on money, drugs, sex, or violence in its rawest form. A lot of these topics are watered down in most musicals because they were made in the beginning and middle of the century, when things were less explicit.

But today's teens can still relate to many of the messages that musicals convey. For instance, in *West Side Story*, Officer Krupke pisses off the Jets gang royally. They want to go out and release their anger violently, which would've sent them straight to the slammer.

Instead, they perform a dance and song, "Cool," which helps them control themselves and avoid getting arrested. It was similar to Michael Jackson's "Beat It" video in terms of attitude and how they would lash out unexpectedly with a "Pow!" or "Bam!"

Even though musicals and music videos have many similarities, kids my age who come from the block would probably never allow themselves to appreciate show tunes unless they're being sampled by rappers. The dudes in my neighborhood and high school are all about rap and r&b. They'd rather listen to rhymes in Japanese than take in alternative styles.

The dudes in my neighborhood would rather listen to rhymes in Japanese than take in alternative styles.

There's a black kid I know who listens to rock bands all the time. But he doesn't tell anyone because he fears being ridiculed by his peers. He expresses his love for alternative music only to his closest friends. Like him, I'm afraid to come out of my creative closet because I want to avoid being mocked.

But it's still unfair. Just because I'm a rough dude who happens to like watching films where people abruptly break into song and dance shouldn't automatically draw people to the conclusion that I'm a freak.

I don't want to be the butt of jokes or to be looked at as pitiful. I don't want people to say, "My life is messed up, but I'm better than the cat who likes musicals."

I just don't get it. If Jay-Z can use parts of *Annie* and *Oliver* in his rhymes, why can't I sing songs from *The King and I* in peace?

The writer was 17 when he wrote this story. He later attended college, studying writing.

Getting Ghetto

By Fred Wagenhauser

Would you be interested to hear another Eminem story about a white kid who's been through so much? White kids trying to be ghetto—it sounds like an "Animorph" book, but it's a reality. I'm white, I live in the projects, I can rap, and all my life I've made friends with danger and deceit.

My roots in "urban culture" started while I was just a kid living in New Jersey with my Aunt Trish and Uncle Lenny. That side of the family was mixed, and threw me into a world of hip-hop and r&b.

I liked rap from the jump. I could vibe the lyrics about how hard it was living in the streets because my family had to scrounge to make ends meet. As for r&b, I loved the way Donell Jones' "Where I Wanna Be" and Musiq Soulchild's "Don't Change" captured love and loss.

Now, my family has never been stereotypically white. By that I mean acting like you got a bad smell under your nose, have never been arrested, have a lot of money, and stay away from the projects. My family is not like that. We don't have money, we're not snobs, and some of us have been in care or locked up.

My brother bangs with the six (rolls with a crew) and he's always in trouble. My mother was in foster care when she was little, and when people meet her they know she's real. One time when I riding in the car with my mom, I put on Power 105 and a Snoop Dogg throwback came on. My mother said, "Oh, this is my sh-t!" and she started to sing along with Snoop and Dre. She's gangsta.

I'm white, I live in the projects, I can rap, and all my life I've made friends with danger and deceit.

When I was 9, we moved from Jersey to Brentwood, on Long Island, where my mom grew up. When I got to the block, all I heard playing was reggae, Spanish music, and of course blazin' hip-hop and r&b. Jersey had been peaceful and quiet, but Brentwood was noisy and crowded and chaotic. I loved it.

When September came, 3rd grade was cool and fun but there was one problem: I was a nerd, from how I talked to how I dressed. My family never really had money like that, so I was in Payless kicks and some Wal-Mart clothes. I was always made fun of.

The next year my mom said I was going to a new school. I was happy. Maybe it would be a new start for me. But again, the same things: I had no gear and I was a nerd. What friends I did make wanted me to change.

"Fred, why do you wear such tight pants?" Harry asked one day. "My mother doesn't have it like that," I told him. I felt embarrassed and annoyed, because it's nobody's business why I dress the way I do. But eventually it started to eat at me on the inside.

I asked my mother if I could get new jeans so I wouldn't get picked on. The next time my family took me shopping, I picked out the baggy jeans instead of the nut huggers. I was so happy because I got more respect.

Then the tables turned. One day at lunch when I was 11 years old, my friends (who were all black and Latino, like most of the kids in my school) told me I was a "wigger." I didn't know what that word meant until Harry told me it was a white person trying to be black. That's when I realized that some of the things I did to fit in are not just stereotypically black, but stereotypically ghetto.

When I was 13 years old, I beat up a kid in my middle school and was sent to a residential treatment center, St. Mary's. In that environment, everyone assumed that since I was white and smart I was a nerd. But when they heard my poetry about my life struggles, it wiped the smirk off their faces.

Then I got sent to a lockdown upstate. I don't like to fight but I will if I have to. So I was fighting a lot just to prove to everyone I wasn't an ass. I felt that because I was white I had to be the toughest and meanest kid on the wing to get respect. I had to learn how to freestyle and battle rap and keep up on the new slang coming in. All this just so I could watch TV in peace.

One time, the whole wing was bored so a few kids started to battle rap. James said, "Come on, Fred, it's just like poetry." I tried and messed up but it was cool so I practiced. I started to speak what was on my mind in front of people.

Those experiences taught me to use my voice. I've always been a really shy person. I'm not good in crowds. In general, I really don't believe in myself. When I found out I could survive in lockdown and that I had a little flow, my confidence rose.

But now that I'm right on the borderline of adulthood, I feel I need to change certain aspects of my ghetto ways. I have to calm down a lot. I get into fights on the regular and in the past six months I've been to the bookings three times. Plus, I don't have a real job, I'm not in school, and I'm on the verge of homelessness. It's real hard.

Sometimes I feel it in my bones that if I don't get out of my neighborhood soon, someone's going to get hurt. I don't want to do that. I want to expand my mind. Learning about hip-hop style and music, and to fight, deal, and battle rap—those are not the only things I want to learn in life.

I'm hoping to take my ass to college far away from the Lowa Deck (the Lower East Side, where I live now). But I wonder if I can go to school far from here, and if I do, am I really going to calm down on the criminal stuff? I'm not gonna sit here and lie that "I'm gonna change" when I don't know if I will.

I want the best of both worlds in the palm of my hand. I want to be able to do my thing on job interviews and amaze college professors with my vast intellect, and on the flip side, walk through the projects because I know mad people from different walks of life.

I felt that because I was white I had to be the toughest and meanest kid on the wing to get respect.

I want to show people color doesn't define me. I want to bring my hunger and the ability to adapt that I got from the streets and apply it to making a straight life. That's my uniqueness. But dealing and getting locked up? Nah. I have to be able to control my anger and get out the damn ghetto.

I fear losing my voice and my confidence. I also fear I might get in too deep and bang, I'm caught up again. But I hope that understanding the dangers that living crooked has in store for me will help me find a new way to stand up and be me.

Fred was 21 when he wrote this story.

Dream Girl

By Rance Scully

It was finally summer. School was out, and my friends and I decided we were going to start hanging out with more girls. None of us understood anything about them.

So we took it upon ourselves to go and find out what they were really like. Don't get me wrong; this wasn't one of those competitions to see who could get the most girls over the summer. Our strategy was to try to be their friends and see what we could learn.

Of the four of us, I was the shyest. I made several attempts at striking up conversations, but none of the girls I wanted to talk to wanted to speak to me. They behaved as if the only reason why I would talk to them was in order to "get some." It was like a crime to be seen talking to any guy who lived in the neighborhood.

Meanwhile, my friends were having the same experience, and after a week or so, it was obvious that this plan of ours was getting us nowhere. Then one day we were hanging out in front of my house when a group of people got out of a car right across the road. Among them was one of the most attractive girls that I had ever seen.

She had jet black hair, a cocoa butter complexion, and eyes that glittered in the brightness of the sun. She didn't seem to have lipstick on, but her lips had this cherry red color about them.

My friends and I all stared at her in awe until she disappeared into the house across the road. For the rest of the day the only thing we spoke about was how pretty she was and how badly we wanted to get to know her. One of my friends said she looked exactly like his "dream girl."

None of us understood anything about girls. So we took it upon ourselves to find out what they were really like.

All at once, I started to regret not having been more friendly with the people that lived in that house. In the weeks that followed I started to see her moving in furniture. I found myself walking by the house just to try to get a glimpse of her. Each time I saw her, I would end up thinking about her for the entire day. I became obsessed.

Soon my friends were teasing me, asking me, "What's up, Rance? Are you in love with this girl?" I would laugh and try to change the subject, but no matter how hard I tried I just couldn't get over talking about her whenever I got the chance.

I really wanted to meet this girl but was too shy to approach her. I would stand in front of my mirror and go over hundreds of things that I would say to her if I ever got the chance. Soon she became the only thing on my mind and I even stopped hanging with my friends. Instead I would sit in my room and draw pictures of hearts and write love letters to her.

My friends called me a coward and threatened to stop hanging with me if I didn't go and talk to her. But I could never seem to gather up the courage.

Then one day when summer was over and I was on my way home from school, I deliberately walked on the side of the road where she lived and saw a guy talking to her. To my surprise it was Paul the player. Paul was this guy who drove a real fancy car and had a new girl in it every day. Every girl living in the vicinity knew what he was after. Why was she talking to him?

At first I wondered if maybe no one had warned her about Paul, but I figured that she ought to be smart enough to see straight through his act.

The next day when I was coming home I saw her talking to yet another guy who was famous for his promiscuous behavior. I started thinking that she must be a chickenhead.

But when she started hanging with some of the girls on the block who had similar reputations to Paul and the other guy, I decided she wasn't stupid—she must be like them. My heart was broken, and yet I had to think realistically. After all, she wasn't my girlfriend. She was free to do whatever she wanted with herself.

I tried my very best to get her off my mind, and after a few weeks I found myself thinking less and less of her. Then one day I was on the bus and almost like a dream she came on board. The only available seat was the one next to me and without hesitation she sat down in it.

I was uncomfortable. I didn't want to have anything to do with her. "Why is this girl sitting beside me?" I thought to myself, as I slowly turned to get a better look at her. I remember being surprised all over again to see how smooth and spotless her skin was and how beautiful she was. I turned my head and stared out the window.

"Why is it that I have always wanted to speak to this girl," I thought, "and it's only now when I am the least interested that

Dream Girl

she is sitting right here next to me?" While these thoughts were racing through my head, I kept looking out the window. Then I heard a voice:

"Hi," she said.

"Hello," I replied nervously.

"Are you the guy who lives on my block?"

I was surprised to find out that she had even noticed me at all. "Yes," I said.

"What's your name?"

"Rance," I said in a suave and sophisticated manner.

"Unusual, but nice," she said. Her name was Kai and she was being awfully friendly. I was suspicious and wondered to myself whether this friendliness had gotten guys like Paul the player everything they wanted.

But as we continued to talk I started to feel more and more at home with her. She told me where she was from and how her mom was ill and in the hospital for a few months, which was why she was living in Brooklyn. Before I knew it we were talking like close friends. All this time, I couldn't help admiring her face, especially her lips.

"Are you this friendly to everyone?" I asked awkwardly. She said she was. "Why?" I asked her.

She smiled. "The only way you can know anything about another person is to converse with them," she said.

She smiled. "The only way you can know anything about another person is to converse with them," she said. "If you don't like what you hear, stop talking to them."

I looked at her and nodded in agreement. I thought I had this girl all figured out, but once I actually spoke to her, she turned out to be completely different than I thought. We talked until we got to our stop and after we got off I walked her to her house and bid her a friendly goodbye.

It wasn't long before she moved out of the neighborhood. But

Look Beyond the Label

even though we eventually lost touch, we continued to talk on the telephone for a while after that. What began as a big crush turned to suspicion and disdain and then to undying admiration. I suppose I did make a female friend after all, a close one. Kai, if you happen to read this, thanks.

Rance was 19 when he wrote this story.

Rappin' With the 5-0

By Allen Francis

Before I decided to do this story, I'd never in my life had any dealings with the police and that was OK with me. I had heard too many stories from family and friends about the brutal nature of cops and seen too many examples of it on the news.

It was all too easy for me to imagine being stopped by a cop one day and hearing those deadly words, "You fit the description of..." The scene would end with the cop beating me over the head with his nightstick while humming his favorite song.

I decided I needed to lighten up a bit. A lot of cops may be brutal or crooked, but not all of them, right? I wanted to find out for myself what cops are really like and experience some of what they have to do on the job. Then I could share whatever I learned with the readers of *NYC*, the teen magazine I write for. So I set out for my neighborhood precinct, the 42nd.

As I got ready to leave the house, my mother told me to put a hat on to cover my braids. I usually wear a bandana, but she says it makes me look like a "hoodlum."

My mom was nervous about me entering police territory but I wasn't. All I was going to do was ask to talk to the youth affairs officer about teen programs in the precinct and the tensions that exist between cops and teenagers. No problem.

As I was walking to the precinct, my enthusiasm started to drain out of me. With each step I thought of better things I could be doing—reading a comic, watching TV, sleeping, bungee jumping, lion taming, anything but this.

As I stopped in front of the station house I was glad I had my hat on. I didn't want to be fighting off cops because I fit the description of some guy with braids who had just robbed a bank or something.

> *I pictured a cop in riot gear yelling, "We need backup, repeat, backup, there's a black guy on the premises!"*

I could see it now, one cop in riot gear yelling, "We need backup, repeat, backup, there's a black guy on the premises!" Swarms of cops busting out of windows and doors, wielding batons that have my name on them, and not a video camera in sight. Man, I really needed to relax.

The first thing I saw when I walked in was a long bench with about four cops sitting on it—just waiting for me. I asked to see the youth affairs officer. They all looked at each other and finally one of them said she was in a conference.

I asked how long she would be busy and was told, "For an hour or two." Oh fiddlesticks, I thought, I wasn't going to get to sit in a police station and interview cops. I was so disappointed, gosh darn the luck.

I wrote out a note asking for an interview. I left my phone number and a copy of *NYC* with the officer behind the desk and asked him to make sure the youth officer got it. He said, "Sure," but something about the way he put the message and magazine down gave me the feeling that the youth officer would never see it.

A few days later I was at it again, trying to find the 10th precinct in Manhattan. (I picked it because it was close to *NYC*'s office.) When I saw the cruisers parked out front, I wiped my brow because I was sweating and took a couple of breaths.

I walked in and saw another long bench with three officers sitting on it. I twisted my tongue in knots trying to explain that I was a teen reporter and wanted to talk to the youth affairs officer.

I was acting all nervous so I tried to cool out. I got into a stance that suggested I felt totally all right standing in a police station, with braids in my hair, wearing an earring and baggy pants.

One of the cops got on the phone for a minute and then gestured for me to go into the room behind him. "Fitzgerald will answer your questions," he said with a smile.

I walked in like a zombie, saying "Uh, Officer Fitzgerald?" It was a small room with three people in it. Fitzgerald pulled up a chair for me and I sat down, going through my robotic routine of explaining my name and what my business was.

The other cops left the office and Fitzgerald stood up. This guy was big. He closed the door with his nightstick and we were alone in this small room. This was it. I imagined *NYC* printing an issue with my face on the cover, with the headline, "In Memory of Allen."

But instead of hitting me with the nightstick, Officer Fitzgerald asked me if I was in high school. When I told him I lived in the Bronx, he told me that his father lived there, too--you know, small talk.

As we got into the interview we would crack a joke here and there. It was amazing—I was relaxing in a squadhouse with the 5-0, the fuzz, the boys in blue. Before I left, Fitzgerald gave me his number and said to call him if he could be of any more help.

Before leaving the precinct, I also met Officer Karen Delancey

77

of youth affairs. She was a beautiful young woman (she told me she had been a model before becoming a cop) who sat down and started talking to me about rap. We were actually rapping songs we both knew in the middle of the police station. Then I remembered I had an interview to do.

I asked her about the tensions between teens and cops, and Officer Delancey talked about how some teens have to show off in front of their friends. They do something wrong, she said, and then they can look cool struggling with the cops or saying they got picked on.

I thought she made a point there, but it wasn't the whole story. Sure there are problem teens but there are also problem cops. I realized that I was uncomfortable around all cops because of the actions of the ones who think they're above the law, the ones who harass or brutalize citizens. I had gotten the idea that all cops are like the ones in the bad headlines.

> **My uneasiness around cops hasn't gone away, but my general dislike of cops has.**

But my experience at the 10th precinct showed me that not every cop is that way. Some like to joke around, like Officer Fitzgerald; others are beautiful ex-models like Officer Delancey. Eventually I got to do my interview at the 42nd precinct and that went smoothly, too.

Before doing this story, my image of a cop was a bad cop, the kind that abuses power. I'd never run into a "good" cop, the kind who stops every once in a while from walking the beat to talk to you. But I know now that there are some out there.

My uneasiness around cops hasn't gone away, but my general dislike of cops has. Now I might dislike individual cops because of their actions, but I won't let that turn me against all of them.

Allen was 18 when he wrote this story. He graduated from college and worked in higher education administration.

Forbidden Territory: The Projects

By Fabiola Duvalsaint

The projects. A year ago I would have shuddered at the thought of visiting one and being around the people who live there. I didn't know anything about public housing projects because I had never been to one. But that didn't stop me from imagining what they were like.

To me, the projects were a place where dangerous people lived, a place you didn't go if you didn't live there. I mean, people in the housing projects are mostly drug dealers and prostitutes, right? Basically, they were forbidden territory.

Now, my neighborhood wasn't the kind with white picket fences up and down the block either. For a while, my neighborhood was thought of as dangerous, but at least it was changing for the better.

The way they made projects look on TV, how could you not be scared? The tall buildings that all look the same, the drug dealers racing to see who could make the quickest sale, and the daily shootings.

If a girl in school passed by with "door knocker" earrings, baggy pants with the boxers hanging out, and a bandanna wrapped around her head, one of my friends would look at her and automatically say, "Here comes the projects." And everyone at our table would burst out laughing.

> **The way they made projects look on TV, how could you not be scared?**

Then I met Maria (not her real name). We met freshman year in gym class, but we weren't really friends. Maria was tall, Hispanic, had wild, curly black hair most girls would die for, and was very blunt. If she didn't like something, she would let you know it in a second. She spoke her mind and didn't care about the consequences.

We had a math class together. One day, I noticed she had a cool blue nail polish, so I asked for the name. She looked at me as if I was stupid and said, "It's blue." After that I was like, "Forget that!"

Then one day a girl dropped her pen in class. When she tried to get it with her foot, she got stuck. Maria and I started laughing. We were laughing so hard that the whole class attention was watching us. After that, we just started talking like two friends who knew each other from way back.

For a while during junior year we got separated. But one day we bumped into each other and decided to meet at McDonald's once a month after school.

Then once a month turned into once a week and, before I knew it, Maria and I were getting together every day, either to hang out at my house or at the school's athletic field.

One day I asked if I could come over to her house.

"You want to come over my house?" she asked, looking like I was talking in a foreign language.

"Yeah," I said. "What's the matter?"

Maria just looked at me and smiled. "I live in the projects," she said. I looked to see if she was kidding, but deep inside I knew she was dead serious. How was I going to get myself out of this situation?

I guess she could tell how I felt by looking at my face, because Maria told me right away that I didn't have to go if I didn't want to. I wanted to back out, I really did, but I sensed that not going would mean my friendship with her wasn't real.

When my last class ended that day, I went to meet Maria at our usual spot (the locker room). As we started to walk, Maria looked at me and started laughing. I asked her what was so funny (because at this point I sure needed a good laugh).

"You're scared to go to the projects!" she said.

I turned toward her and looked her straight in the face. "I'm not scared. Why should I be?"

Great! Not only was I a coward, but I'd turned into a liar, too. I wanted to turn back, and had almost decided to, but just then Maria pointed to an orange building surrounded by other orange buildings.

When I looked around I was shocked. There were no drug dealers on the corners and I certainly didn't hear any gunshots.

"Here it is," she said.

I had been so filled with dread and my thoughts were so locked on turning back that I didn't even realize that we had already arrived.

When I looked around I was shocked. There were no drug dealers on the corners and I certainly didn't hear any gunshots. This neighborhood was quiet and calm—as if all the people who lived here were hibernating inside their apartments. Was this what I was afraid of?

We crossed the street and went inside her building. When we got upstairs to her apartment, I met her mom and sister. I got so comfortable in her apartment that my fears melted away. My worries were all just gone!

Her apartment was like any other and her room was just as messy as mine, which made me even more comfortable. She had a dog named Rufus that tried to kill me when he saw me and a quiet cat that just sat around. Her mom looked harmless.

When it was time to leave, I told her that this time I really wasn't scared and I could manage to get to the bus stop across the street on my own. After that day I went over to Maria's house often.

Now I've grown to learn the true meaning of the saying, "Believe none of what you hear and half of what you see." And I am not as ignorant as I used to be.

Fabiola was 18 when she wrote this story. She graduated from college and became a magazine editor and freelance journalist.

No, I Don't Have a Pet Lion

By Aissata Kebe

"Do you raise lions and monkeys as pets in Africa?"

When a boy in my 11th grade English class asked me that question, I was so angry and surprised that I didn't know what to say. Why would someone ask such a silly question about my beautiful continent? I told him that I'd only seen lions and monkeys when I went to the zoo with my family.

I'm from Dakar, the capital city of Senegal, a country in West Africa. The only animals we raise as pets are cats and dogs. Some people like to raise chickens, and in the smaller villages in the country, some raise cows and sheep. Wild lions are rare in West Africa and monkeys only live in the wild.

It hurts to know that so many people are clueless about Africa. And I am especially disappointed that my classmates—most of whom are also immigrants from other countries—have ignorant ideas about the continent. Africa isn't just the images of wild animals and poor and sick people you see on TV. It's a beautiful continent with 53 countries and hundreds of different languages.

Luckily, I wasn't the only African student in my class at Brooklyn International High School in New York. My friend Tidiane is from Guinea in West Africa, and he told me not to bother answering stupid questions. He said sometimes he answers by making up scary things about Africa, saying it's all one big jungle with elephants and many dangerous animals.

But it's not just high school students who ask ignorant questions. My cousin Bachire, who came to the United States to attend college, also gets asked ridiculous questions. His classmates asked him how he got here, maybe thinking that we don't have airplanes in Africa. My cousin told them that he swam the Atlantic Ocean to the U.S., and he said they believed him.

When I arrived in New York for medical treatment in 2001, I was surprised at how little the people here knew about Africa. One day at my sister's hair braiding shop on Nostrand Avenue in Brooklyn, one of her clients asked us if we wear shoes in Africa.

Of course Africans wear shoes! In Dakar, people wear Nikes, Jordans and other brand names. It irritates me that people think that Africa is still what it was 200 years ago. Everything you can buy here in the U.S., we can buy in Senegal.

Still, when people have questions about Africa, I think it's better to answer them—or at least not make up ridiculous answers. Telling lies doesn't help educate them about the place I love. So when people in the U.S. ask questions, I try to change the way they think by teaching them about my life there.

One day, I brought pictures of my city in Senegal to school. I told my classmates that more than 2 million people live in Dakar, which has tall modern apartment and office buildings. There are cafés and clubs that pick up once the sun goes down.

The students in my English class couldn't believe that these were images of Africa. They all started saying, "Is this Africa?"

"I thought it was like a jungle with elephants and other wild animals!" one student said. "I will tell my father so that I can go and visit there one day!"

I told her that she was welcome to go to our house in Senegal anytime she wanted to. I made the offer because my family is generous, although that isn't unusual in Senegal. Senegal's nickname is "Reewu Teranga," which means "generous country" in my language, Wolof.

We like to welcome people to our homes and give them something to eat. I can visit and eat at any of my neighbors' houses anytime. It's a tradition for rich people to help the poor by giving them money and food.

When my cousin's classmates asked how he got to the U.S., he told them that he swam the Atlantic Ocean. They believed him.

Because my family is relatively well off, we've been able to help other people. When I was about 8, a lady who neither my mom nor my dad knew used to come to our house and we gave her food, water, and clothes to wear.

After many years, she became like family and started calling my mom her sister-in-law. Calling someone your sister-in-law or your sister, even though they aren't, isn't unusual in Senegal.

Sometimes such generosity can be too much. When it's time to eat, you must eat no matter what because your host will keep insisting until you do. That has happened to me so many times and I hate it, because sometimes I don't feel like eating and they won't let me be.

People eat sitting on mats on the floor with their legs crossed, eating with their hands from big shared plates. We eat *thieb bou dienn* (rice and fish with vegetables) and *yassa* (chicken cooked with onion sauce mixed with white rice).

I know there is great poverty in Africa. Not all rich people help the poor. We need more government aid to feed people and get them jobs. But that's not all there is to say about my beautiful continent.

Although it bothers me that people don't know all the good things about my country, I can't really blame them for thinking the way they do. What they see on TV influences what they think about Africa. If they're not watching shows about lions and antelopes on the Discovery Channel or Animal Planet, they're seeing programs about the ugly parts of the continent and the most hungry and sick people.

I understand how misleading TV can be. It influenced what I thought about the U.S. before I got here. When I was in Senegal, I watched a lot of American movies, including *Home Alone* and *American Pie*, and TV shows like *Baywatch*. Those programs made me believe that the U.S. was the most perfect country in the world. I thought it was a place where people partied a lot, where everyone was rich and there weren't any homeless people.

American TV shows made me believe that everyone in the U.S. was rich and there weren't any homeless people.

I didn't know that many people here are immigrants or the children of immigrants from all over the world. I didn't know that there are a lot of poor people and that there are ghettos. I started to learn more about the U.S. when I was 11, after two college students from Wisconsin came to live with us for six months. We gave them Senegalese names: Aicha and Biguee.

They told us that the U.S. wasn't like we imagined. They said that in the U.S., "time is money" and that everyone is busy. When I came here at age 13, I saw that they were right and that life in the U.S. can be hard. The myths I'd believed about the U.S. were shattered.

After being here for four years, I've learned that the U.S. can be a hard place for everyone, especially immigrants. You can't get money when you don't work. Getting to know the country and learning the language is very difficult. Life in the U.S. can be pleasant sometimes because of the tremendous opportunities, but it's hard for many immigrants.

If I go back to Senegal after living in the U.S. for a while, I'll get to teach other people who didn't get the chance to come here. I'll teach them about the good and the bad parts of living here, because I don't want them to be disappointed if they come here. I also think my experience in the U.S. will help me to be more open-minded when it comes to other countries.

And as long as I live here, I realize I'll always have to teach people about my country. So the next time someone asks me if we wear shoes or live with animals in Africa, I will sit them down and show them pictures of me in Africa. Hopefully, the more I teach, the fewer people will ask those kinds of questions.

Aissata was 19 when she wrote this story. She graduated from high school in New York.

He's Black, I'm Asian

By Priscilla Chan

It all began on a Friday afternoon. A friend and I were at a meeting for Red Cross volunteers. Because the volunteers came from different schools, the kids in charge thought we all should participate in an icebreaker to get to know each other a little better. Each participant was supposed to select a card with one item of a set written on it and search the room for his/her match. My friend chose Bacon, but she never found Eggs. I chose Beauty, and to my dismay, very quickly found Beast.

See, I hate icebreakers. I figure, if I really wanted to make friends with the other people in this room, I'd do it on my own terms. I don't need anyone telling me, "Here, do this exercise and you'll make friends."

I was planning on subtly tossing aside my card and pretending that I'd never selected one. The card was floating to the ground; I was going to get away with it. Then, all of a sudden, some guy snatches it in mid-air: "Hey, look! I'm your match!" After suppressing a grimace, I decided to give him a try. "How bad could it be?" I thought.

So there we were. I was Asian. He was black. I wore a loose shirt and jeans and my hair up. He wore baggy clothing and his hair in dreads. I was quiet and basically passive. From him emanated an aura of "street smarts" and "hoodiness." He was about two heads taller and two times wider than me. He absolutely personified what I thought to be the typical black teenager.

He walked with a little hop-step to meet me, seeming actually excited, while I dragged myself over to him with a stoic look on my face.

It was uncanny how much we had in common. I have to admit I was surprised.

He seemed to command the room with the very way he walked and presented himself. Meanwhile, I was trying to sink into the floor so I wouldn't have to put myself through this. "What am I going to have in common with this guy?" I wondered.

The first words that came out of his mouth after we sat down merely reinforced my belief that we would have nothing in common. As soon as we sat down—even before the introductions, even before the awkward hellos—he asked me, "Have you ever gone out with someone before?"

I was so taken aback. My mouth just dropped open, and I must have looked like an idiot waiting for flies to come in. I wasn't prepared for anything even remotely like this question to come up in our conversation. I guess he must have realized this because right after that, he said, "Hey, don't worry about it. My name's Rex."

Rex and I talked for a really long time. He would ask me something, and then I'd answer it. My answer would spark another question and the answer to that would bring up another topic for discussion.

Look Beyond the Label

Surprisingly, I didn't have any regrets after our conversation started. In fact, I was intrigued. He was very open, and we didn't once feel awkward with what we were talking about.

We learned we both liked to watch football, but we loved playing baseball; our best subjects were math and we both hated history; and we were very much alike in our experiences and our goals. We both wanted to become professionals in the field of science and technology. It was uncanny how much we had in common.

I have to admit that I was surprised, even though I knew that it's wrong to judge a book by its cover. That it's wrong to stereotype people. That it's wrong to picture someone as a color or "type."

I don't know where the majority of my stereotypes came from, but I can assume they were either handed down to me from my mother, or passed on to me by my friends and acquaintances. Or maybe I just observed some things myself.

Well, wherever they came from, I had the basic ones in my mind when I met Rex. Blondes have more fun. Guys are more outgoing than girls. And black guys who act like they're "all that" are hoody and care more about girls than their grades. Yes, there was a time when I believed these things. I guess I believed them because I didn't have many black (or blonde) friends to negate my beliefs.

Rex and I started talking about stereotypes because we both believed they were a big problem among people our age. I had an image not only of the typical black teenager, but of the typical Asian teenager as well. Rex said he didn't really have any concrete stereotypes, so he wanted me to tell him all about mine—to "amuse" him, he said.

In trying to get him to see that I wasn't the stereotypical Asian, I said that I wasn't like other Asians because I didn't wear clothes from The Gap, I didn't own three pairs of Docks, I didn't have a keen interest in spending hours on end in a smoky pool hall, I didn't enjoy playing Ultimate Frisbee, and a score of other things. Rex pointed across the auditorium at a group of Asian girls:

"So, they typical to you?" he asked.

"Yes, most definitely."

"Why?"

"'Cause like I just said, all their stuff is so preppy and so typical of what they would wear. I bet they just came from the pool hall down the street."

"Well, that one over there, she's not wearing Docks," Rex pointed out. "And the one next to her, she's wearing a dress. You can't play Ultimate in no dress. You can't say that all of them are typical."

"Oh, for today, they're just exceptions," I replied. "Any other day, they'd be typical."

"So you're saying that any other day, they'd be interchangeable with each other 'cause they're all typical?" Rex asked.

"Well, no," I said. "I mean, I'm sure that they're different people, but—"

> *"So, how can you say they're all typical if they're all different?" Rex raised his hands in an "I-just-busted-you" gesture.*

"So, how can you say they're all typical if they're all different?" His eyebrows shot up about half-an-inch and he raised his hands in an "I-just-busted-you" gesture. The corner of his lip curled up and he smiled. "Now you see?"

Rex and I had been talking for about 20 minutes when we had to stop because the Red Cross meeting was starting. By this time, he and I knew so much about each other. We liked the same sports; we cared a lot about our grades; we both had been mugged. Almost everything we talked about we had in common.

I was sad that it was over but glad at the same time. I had made a good friend by doing the icebreaker and didn't want to stop talking with him, but I felt like it was enough for one day. I said a quick goodbye, thinking we were never going to speak to each other again. But one of the things that we had in common brought us together once more.

We had both gotten selected as chairpersons of committees in the Red Cross. Although we didn't get picked for the same committee, we still saw each other at committee update meetings. And that's where we continued our unusual friendship.

The more I got to know Rex, the more I saw that he wasn't stereotypical at all. In fact, he got me to realize that there are no typical black teens, or any other kind of teens. Looking back, the conversations that Rex and I had with each other really did make a difference in our lives. He showed me enough to disprove my stereotypes, and I showed him much to give him hope that people can change. He was able to combat my ignorance. It took a few minutes before I realized he was for real, but once I got to listening, everything about him just opened up, and I began to hear things that ultimately changed my thinking.

I try not to think in terms of stereotypes anymore. Now, I can't believe I ever thought that way. Sometimes I have a relapse here and there, but I don't think of things being typical anymore, and I have Rex to thank for my epiphany.

It's hard to believe that one person can change your whole way of thinking, but Rex was that person for me. Now, walking down streets, I look at people and marvel, "What hidden things are there about this person that I would have missed had I judged him by the way he looks?"

Priscilla was 18 when she wrote this story. She graduated from college and graduate school and became, among other things, the dean of a middle school and a writer for the New York Times Learning Network.

She's Cool, She's Funny, She's Gay

By Sandra Leon

When I was younger, I never really cared about what other people had to say about homosexuals. But ever since my sister Sonia "came out of the closet," I've been defensive about the topic. Now I can't let the dumb remarks I hear about gay people go by without commenting on them.

Now, every time I bring friends to my house, Sonia is the first person I introduce them to. When they leave I tell them, "That's my sister—the one who is gay." Some of my friends just say, "Oh, she's the one? Well, she's nice." But others do a double-take: "That's her? No way, get out of here, really?!"

The people who are surprised tell me that Sonia doesn't look gay or that she doesn't act like a gay person. I reply, "What does a gay person look like? How are they supposed to act?" After that, all they have left to say is: "Well, you know." I tell them, "No, I don't know" and ask them to explain themselves.

As a result, I've gotten into some heavy conversations about gay stereotypes with my friends. I couldn't believe some of the ideas they had about gay people. They told me that gay women dress and look masculine. That they act like men because that's what they want to be. Since my sister isn't like that, she couldn't be gay as far as they were concerned.

I tell them that their stereotypes just aren't true. As far as I know, my sister loves being a woman. She enjoys her femininity. Her being gay does not have anything to do with a secret desire to be a man—far from it. Sonia is gay because she enjoys the company of other women, physically as well as mentally. She's told me that, for her, a relationship between two women is deeper than that of a woman and a man.

Another thing that a lot of my friends believe is that gay people try to get straight people to become gay. Once a friend asked if she could stay at my house for a couple of days. I told her she could stay as long as she wanted, but she must be comfortable with my sister. She said, "OK, as long as Sonia doesn't fall in love with me." I thought that was a very stupid thing for her to say. My sister doesn't chase after straight women. So I replied with sarcasm: "You're not her type, so please, darling, don't flatter yourself."

A lot of my friends believe that gay people try to get straight people to become gay.

Some of my friends also feel that gay people have a negative view of the opposite sex. Not true. My sister has always had men for best friends. Just because she is not attracted to them sexually does not mean that she hates men.

I've found out that even a lot of people who condemn discrimination based on race or religion or nationality act like discrimination against gay people is acceptable. Why is that? How can you be open-minded about one aspect of a person and close-minded about another? Even people who have been victims of discrimination themselves can be totally insensitive when it comes to gay people.

I don't understand people like that, but I can give them a piece of advice: open your minds, your ears, and your hearts. My mother has and so have a lot of my friends. Knowing Sonia has taught them that you can't believe stereotypes.

Sandra was 18 when she wrote this story. She later graduated from college.

A Classmate in a Wheelchair

By Esther Rajavelu

I first saw him freshman year, rolling by in his wheelchair. His short arms rested on the desktop attached to his chair. He had dark hair, a frozen smile, and he stared straight ahead. He didn't seem to look anyone in the eye. "They let people like that in Brooklyn Tech?" I thought.

One day, I was standing in the hall with some other kids waiting for our history class to begin when he rolled up. I felt myself stiffen and I wanted to get away from him, but I couldn't. I didn't want to hurt his feelings by moving. But I also didn't want to embarrass myself by being seen next to him. I had the urge to say something, but my mind was blank.

Finally, I glanced at him and decided to smile. He looked at me as if I were a ghost and tried to smile back. That surprised me. I thought he would just ignore me. I quickly looked away, wish-

A Classmate in a Wheelchair

ing the teacher would come so I could rush into class.

Then I noticed everybody else was quiet, too. It hit me that I wasn't the only one who felt creepy when he was around. Nearly everyone's attitude changed when he entered class. The chatter stopped and kids looked the other way. Even the teachers ignored him. It was like they wanted to erase him from the class. I wondered what was behind this weird feeling.

I began to realize how uncomfortable and afraid I feel around disabled people. After all, before high school, the only people I ever saw in wheelchairs were in the movies. Because I didn't really know anyone who was disabled, I got all my ideas from family, friends, and TV.

I realized how uncomfortable and afraid I feel around disabled people.

I definitely believe that the stories I've heard about disabled people influenced the way I felt around them. For instance, the day I smiled at the boy in the wheelchair, I came home and told my mom about it.

"I don't know why he looked at me so weird," I said.

"Well, he probably felt uncomfortable in his position," my mom said. "I don't think it's a good idea for you to get too friendly with him. People like that could get possessive because they're always lonely, and he might try and take advantage of you." Then she told me she read a magazine article about a disabled man who killed his best friend for wanting to spend less time together.

That made me think twice about becoming friends with him. For most of the next year, I listened to my mom's advice. Whenever the boy in the wheelchair was around, I just ignored him. If I saw him in the hall or in class, I turned my head.

Then, during my junior year, I was walking around my government class selling candy bars for the debate team, but nobody was buying. When I walked past the boy in the wheelchair, I heard a murmur that sounded like a request for candy. I was so shocked that I wasn't even sure if he had spoken.

I stood there gaping for a moment and then handed him two bars. From under his desk he got two dollars and gave it to me. I walked back to my desk in amazement.

Later, I realized that when I was going around the classroom asking everybody else if they wanted candy, I hadn't even thought to ask him. I just didn't think he ate candy, or anything else that my friends and I liked. I thought he was too different.

After this, I really wanted to learn how to act around him. A part of me wanted to be extra-friendly, but in my heart I knew I would feel like a fraud. Even now, I'm afraid of what my friends might think if I started hanging out with him. But ignoring him didn't work either, because I still felt uncomfortable whenever he was around.

I started to deal with that "weird" feeling I get around disabled people. I tried to be very honest about my feelings and stereotypes, and I asked a lot of questions. I think it paid off, because my attitude began to change a little. Now I know there's more to being around people with disabilities than feeling pity.

Esther was 17 when she wrote this story. She went to college and graduate school and works for a financial company.

Why No One Knows I'm a Foster Child

By Shaniqua Sockwell

Do you know how it feels to see other couples walk past you embracing, hugging, and kissing, and not get that same kind of affection for yourself?

Believe me, I do! But I'm not the only one, a lot of teenagers feel the same way. It comes to the point that unless you're "hooked up," you're stuck in a lonely situation for a while.

But this story isn't just about being lonely because you're not "hooked up." It's about being lonely because you won't give affection to someone you like because that person may find out something about you that will, from his perspective, ruin the relationship completely.

This thing is finding out you're a foster child. None of my friends know that I am one.

Look Beyond the Label

I remember when my little sister almost blew my cover. (This has nothing to do with relationships, but you'll understand what I'm getting at.) I brought a female friend over to my foster home once and my little sister came into the living room and asked me for something. While I was getting it, my friend looked at my foster mother's wedding album and said, "You don't look like your parents at all." My little sister said, "That's because they're not our..."

> *I told my little sister never to tell anyone that we are foster kids, because we won't be treated the same way as everyone else.*

I didn't even have to guess what was going to come out of her mouth next. I ran in the living room, covered her mouth, excused us, and gave her a verbal lashing. I told her never to tell anyone that we are foster kids, because we won't be treated the same way as everyone else. She gave me this "Are-you-crazy?!" look, but she agreed. That was the last time I ever brought friends to my house.

Hiding my identity, especially from my friends, is difficult. You don't know how many stories and lies I've told people. I've had to lie about why me and my foster sister look nothing alike, about why I never talk about my family much, and about how I suddenly appeared in my home out of nowhere at the age of 10.

I remember when some of my friends were talking about their families. They asked me about my family and how I liked living in the Bronx (they knew that I had moved to Brooklyn from the Bronx, but they didn't know why). I told them I felt sick and excused myself. They never asked me about my family again. The reason I didn't say anything about my family was because I felt that they would judge me because of what had happened in my past.

Now, the situation with boys. Hiding my situation from boys is even harder than hiding it from friends. They usually want to know about everything and if you get touchy about a certain thing, they'll start going off on you. That's why I make sure I don't get touchy, I just avoid their questions.

I remember once I was talking to a boy who I thought understood me. I think he knew something was wrong, because when he asked me questions like, "Why don't you talk about your family or nuthin'?" I would get scared and change the subject. (That's one of the things that makes me feel bad—I want people to understand me but I'm also afraid to get too close.)

He was the first boy I was going to tell I was a foster kid, but I soon came to realize that his concern about my situation was nothing but an act. I caught him talking behind my back one day. I didn't confront him. Instead, I walked away from him and never said anything else to him again. I realized how important trust is in a relationship, especially when you're in foster care.

Then there was Jonathan, who was nosy and went so far as to ask my foster mother why I had suddenly arrived in my family. Jonathan asked my foster mother more questions and finally one day I told him that if he couldn't mind his own business, he could leave. I lost his friendship because I didn't want to answer questions about my past.

My feelings about holding everything inside haven't changed that much during the six years I've been in care. There are times when I think if I don't tell everyone I'm a foster child, I'll go crazy. But if I do, I'm afraid that people will label me and say things like, "She's nobody special; she's just a foster kid."

I want people to understand me but I'm also afraid to get too close.

I'm very lonely and this has its ups and downs. The up is that you don't get your heart broken by someone who doesn't understand what you've been through. The down is that you don't experience firsthand the feeling of caring for someone in a loving way.

Look Beyond the Label

Although I'm still not able to tell people I'm a foster child, I've learned a valuable lesson: if someone can't accept you for who you are, they're not worth the heartache and pain. Someone who really cares for you will come along and you won't be afraid to tell that person you're a foster child. It may take a while, but it will happen.

Shaniqua was 17 when she wrote this story.
She later worked in retail.

The Lowdown on Aisle Seven

By Tony Cedor

In my junior year of high school I started my first job, at a grocery store in Brooklyn, New York.

I worked in the produce section as a part-timer. My job was to keep the fruit and vegetable stand full. I would put the new fruits or vegetables under the old ones so the old ones wouldn't go bad. I also made the salad for the salad bar and had to keep my section clean.

At first I thought that I could work there for a long time—not make a career out of it, but stay a good two or three years. It wasn't in my neighborhood so I didn't have any friends there. No one would be able to distract me while I was working, not like I used to distract some of my friends who worked in McDonald's or Burger King.

After I'd worked there for a while I noticed how every time

a black customer came in I'd hear "88-88" over the loudspeaker. When I asked Joval, who worked with me in the produce section, what "88" meant, he told me it was a code the assistant manager used to notify the staff that a black person had entered the supermarket and should be followed because she might be a shoplifter.

> **"88" was a code the assistant manager used to notify the staff that a black person had entered the supermarket.**

That made me angry because the assistant manager was black himself and wasn't supposed to be doing things like this.

One day, an old black lady came in the supermarket. She looked decent enough, but Bill, the assistant manager, came to me and told me to follow her. I said no.

I told him that it wasn't my job to follow people around and try to catch them stealing. I knew that he couldn't fire me because I was in the union. He just went and got somebody else to do it.

I used to see blacks in decent clothing get followed around to see if they would steal anything, and I'd also see white crackheads come in the supermarket all raggedy looking and stinking the place up, but no one followed them. And most of the people who got caught shoplifting? They were white.

Tony was 18 when he wrote this story. He later graduated from college.

Unwelcome in the Hood

By George Yi

When I was about 9 years old, my father bought a candy store in Bay Ridge, Brooklyn. My family worked in the store and lived there too. I used to sleep in a small room in the back that had an uncomfortable bed.

Knowing that we were about the only Chinese family in the area, I expected mistreatment from the people around there. Most of our new neighbors were Italian and I had heard rumors that Italians didn't really like Asians. I expected to live lonely and remain a prisoner inside the store.

Then, about a week after I moved to Bay Ridge, I saw two Italian kids sitting on a stoop around the block. They approached me and greeted me nicely. We became good friends; in fact, they were my best friends at the time. We'd play all day long with our G.I. Joes and Superman toys and have fun. I felt no racism from these kids or their parents. They made me feel welcome. For the two years I lived there, I was content.

When I was 11, my dad told me that we were going to move again. I agreed to go with him to look at the new house one weekend, to see how I liked it.

We took the train to 225th Street in the Bronx. The neighborhood, located near the Hudson River, was calm and serene. It seemed as if the only thing I could hear was the water floating by.

I saw our new house and its front yard. It looked very appealing. Inside, there were three different rooms, all large, at least much larger than the store space. I liked the place and its quiet environment. I wanted to live there.

My dad let me go for a walk to explore the neighborhood. I went down to the corner grocery store and found a group of older black teenagers hanging around on the street. As I passed them, I heard one of them say, "Ch-nk."

I was infuriated. No one had ever said that to me before. I wanted to punch one of them, but I refrained. I wasn't afraid of them; I just didn't want to throw the first punch. I continued walking but my fists were ready for action. I was ready to fight them if they came after me.

Every time I walked through the streets, I felt my blood pressure rise.

Suddenly, a younger black boy, about 6 years old, came up to me and started talking to me in a fake Chinese accent. He muttered a lot of gibberish. That got me real mad. Why do people have to make fun of someone's language just because they don't understand it? I wanted to hit that kid so badly; I wanted to punch him till he hit the floor. But I didn't. I maintained my composure and walked past him as if nothing had happened.

I was not prepared for this. I had never been insulted that way before. When I got home, I decided not to tell my parents. I thought about it and decided it was a personal matter. I also didn't want them to worry about me.

But that walk changed my perception of the neighborhood from a tranquil place to a place where racism was in your face. During the move from Brooklyn to the Bronx, I felt pain. As I carried box after box into my new home, I felt the life drain away from me.

Life in the new neighborhood was frustrating. I felt alone and left out. I was constantly confronting racism and stereotypes. It seemed like every time I passed some black teenagers, I saw expressions of hatred for me on their faces.

One time at the train station, on my way to school, I saw three towering black figures standing in my way. I said, "Excuse me." They slowly moved away but gave me a really mean look—as if I had physically hurt their parents. As I walked away, they turned around immediately and started to talk that fake Chinese gibberish. I walked up the stairs to the elevated train station and didn't turn back. They kept taunting me and trying to make me angry. When I didn't respond, they spoke louder. I just kept walking with an empty feeling in my bones.

It was upsetting that I had to live in a neighborhood that didn't accept me because of my skin color and facial features. Every time I walked through the streets, I felt my blood pressure rise. So, every chance I got, I tried to leave the Bronx to go somewhere else. Since I went to school in Manhattan, I would stay there or go to a schoolmate's house.

One day, a year after I had moved to the Bronx, I decided to do something different. It was a very nice day out and none of my school friends wanted to do anything. So I decided to walk around the neighborhood. I was determined to ignore the racist people and have fun.

I walked down 225th Street and entered a pizza shop. The pizza smelled good and fresh, so I decided to buy a slice. Inside, I saw a bunch of black and Hispanic teenagers getting slices and playing arcade games in the back. I ate my pizza and headed for the back room to play a game. The other teenagers gave me a deep stare as I approached the machines. I saw one Black kid playing Street Fighter II, one of my favorite games, so I decided to challenge him. 'Would you mind if I join in?" I asked. He responded, "No. No problem."

I inserted my quarter. The two of us ended up playing for hours, until we ran out of money.

Although we were game fighting, we were also making friends. I asked him his name, and he told me it was Andrew. After that day, we continued meeting at the pizza place, bringing more and more quarters each time. After a while, we decided to do other things together, like bike riding. We would race up to 20 blocks without stopping, not even for cars. We rode around until day turned to night.

Andrew respected me. He never made fun of me or insulted my race. He even supported me at times when other people disrespected me. One time when Andrew and I were walking near my house we saw two black kids, one older than me and one younger (I think they were brothers). Andrew quickly stood in front of me as we approached them. The boys started to speak the gibberish that was supposed to sound like Chinese. Andrew said, "Shut up. Don't you got something better to do than insult a Chinese kid?" They shut up and didn't speak another word. I was glad to know that someone was my right-hand man for a change.

I've learned that you can't let a few bad experiences turn you against a whole group of people.

After getting to know Andrew, I met other black and Hispanic kids around the parks and the arcade. We all got along just fine. I finally felt welcome in my neighborhood. On weekends, I would go hang out with my new friends, play at the arcades, and ride my bike through the streets. I no longer had to choose between staying trapped in my house or leaving the Bronx. I felt more free and more lively. Some teenagers around the neighborhood still made racial remarks to me, but it didn't bother me as much anymore. I knew that not everyone was against me.

After three years of living in the Bronx, my family moved again. Now, I live in Chinatown. Sometimes it feels like a safe haven, living in a mostly Asian neighborhood. I immediately felt like I belonged.

After the way I was harassed when I first moved to the Bronx, I developed a stereotype that all black people were bad and looking for trouble. I'd see some black kids walking around in their hooded clothing and baggy jeans, and think that they were looking for some Chinese kids to pick on. Day after day, I would expect to hear insults and fake Chinese accents from people who didn't know me.

It took my friendship with Andrew to show me that not all black people fit that stereotype. I've learned that you can't let a few bad experiences turn you against a whole group of people. You have to keep an open mind.

Although I haven't kept in touch with my friends in the Bronx, I have made new friends—of all races—at my school. I'm glad that I've gotten to know some black and Hispanic people firsthand instead of just hearing stereotypes about them from my Chinese friends. It gives me a better perspective on the world. I've stopped judging people based on their race; now I try to get to know them as individuals.

George was 16 when he wrote this story.

Long-Distance Patriot

By Miranda Neubauer

I'm an American citizen who has spent most of her life in Bielefeld, Germany. My mother's from New York City and we visit relatives there twice a year. Even in Germany I grew up with American children's books like *The Little Engine That Could* and movies like *The Lion King* and loved American culture. I also thought of the U.S. as a land of freedom and equality.

George W. Bush became president in January 2001, when I was in the 8th grade. Until that time, I had a very positive view of America and don't think I would've understood any criticism of it. But I hadn't thought much about what patriotism or loyalty to a country meant.

Before Bush was president, Germans had a more positive, although not great, view of America. The anti-American sentiment in Germany began in early 2001, when the United States would not approve an international treaty to reduce greenhouse gases that contribute to global warming. Germany and more than 100 other countries backed the treaty, called the Kyoto Protocol, but Bush refused.

This made Germans angry because the U.S. is the largest producer of greenhouse gases and the treaty would only be valid if enough countries producing such gases approved it. I was mad when Bush backed out of the treaty and I couldn't understand why he wouldn't want to protect the environment.

This was the first time I became aware that the U.S. government could act against my interests. Since I believe in protecting the environment, I felt confused and hurt, and I didn't really know how to feel about America anymore.

When Bush canceled a treaty with Russia that was supposed to keep both countries from developing certain weapons, Germans were upset again. Like many Germans, I thought the treaty was a good way to minimize the chance of war.

First I just read negative articles in the press, but soon my accordion teacher and the more politically-interested kids at school would ask me questions or make remarks about Bush. Why had Americans elected this president? Were they stupid? Was Bush stupid?

Not all Americans were driving around with guns, eating fast food, and killing the environment.

I never knew what to say. Should I defend a government I didn't agree with? Say nothing? Say, "Well, my mom didn't vote for him?" These were my usual responses, but none seemed right.

I wanted to defend the America I knew and loved: a country where the laws guaranteeing freedom of expression and religion are taken very seriously, a country where people of all different nationalities are accepted, a country with a strong democracy.

I didn't want to argue with my friends, because I was afraid I'd ruin our friendship or the argument would get too heated.

I explained that I didn't agree with the Bush policies, but that didn't help because some people just said, "Well, you're different," and continued criticizing America.

I couldn't stand the broad generalizations many Germans made, such as that all Americans supported Bush or that Americans were only interested in money and controlling the world. They didn't seem to care or want to know that not all Americans were cowboys from Texas, driving around with guns, eating fast food, and killing the environment.

The anti-Americanism around me made examine my own views. There were so many aspects of America that I loved, yet I was also becoming aware of more disturbing parts of American history, such as the Vietnam War. We had invaded a country that hadn't hurt us. We killed many innocent people and many Americans died. It was painful for me to realize that America could be so positive and so negative at the same time.

The questions and my own worries became even more common after the terrorist attacks of September 11th, 2001, which shocked and horrified me.

In the first few days, people in my German school were generally sympathetic, and our school placed a candle commemorating the victims at the entrance.

But shortly after the attacks, one of my teachers started making long speeches presenting the U.S. as all-powerful and almost evil, and implied that it had no culture or only a superficial one. He called the U.S. hypocritical, asking why they were upset about planes flying into the World Trade Center but accepted planes flying over Afghanistan and bombing that country.

While I knew by then that America wasn't perfect and had also made mistakes, I felt his generalizations were just plain wrong and unfair. Whenever he made his speeches, I couldn't stand to look at him and just stared at the floor or my watch, hoping the lesson would be over soon.

I felt like sticking him in a closed room with Fox News and

"The Star-Spangled Banner" constantly playing, but I didn't say anything because I didn't want to get in trouble or harm my grade in his class.

Kids who loved the Internet, Coca-Cola, jeans, and pop music—all parts of American culture—would also compare the U.S. to a big bully telling all the other countries what to do. "America is slowly taking over the world," said one classmate. They accused the U.S. of killing off cultural variety and making every place the same with McDonald's, Wal-Mart, and Hollywood movies.

I realized it's OK to be proud of what's positive about your country, as long as you're honest about the negative.

I found myself partly agreeing with them, partly disagreeing, and just feeling generally confused. I completely disagreed with the terrorists, but I had to wonder what it was about the U.S. that drove them to do such a horrible act of violence.

These thoughts also made me even angrier at Bush. Now whenever he did something that was unpopular in other countries, I felt like he was putting the country at risk.

I tried not to let the anti-Americanism get to me, but one argument with an acquaintance almost brought me to tears. I felt like some of the kids at school were channeling their dislike of the U.S. at me, which made me angry. I began to feel uncomfortable discussing America at all around other kids because I didn't want to bluntly criticize it nor did I feel comfortable praising it.

Bush's threats against Iraq, in late 2002, were very unpopular in the German population and the media. I was upset by the generalizations I heard about war-crazy Americans, especially since the Americans I knew, here and in New York, didn't think the U.S. should invade Iraq.

At the same time, I felt surprised and offended when, after 9/11, some Republicans said that criticizing the U.S. government was the same as being against the U.S. in general. If they wanted to experience anti-Americanism, they should have come to Germany.

A few weeks before the war began, a group of about 15 Americans in Bielefeld, including me and my mother, got together and wrote a statement for the local paper. We wanted to make it clear that we didn't agree with Bush and that not all Americans were for the war.

Soon after we sent the letter, a reporter from the paper interviewed us and wrote an article to accompany the letter. Writing the letter and being featured in the article was important to me. Even though kids in my class didn't comment much on the article, I felt that it did lift the stereotype of the typical American.

I'd never really thought much about patriotism before. But as an American in Germany after 9/11, I slowly came to the opinion that it's OK to be proud of the positive aspects of your country, as long as you're honest about the negative aspects. One can be honest by admitting that there is a problem and then trying to fix it.

It's difficult to define what loyalty to a country means. I think one should respect whoever is in office, but that doesn't mean blindly supporting them.

I am still proud that America is a diverse country, a strong democracy, and that it has an active press. I also love American books, movies, TV, and the generally more relaxed American culture. But I agree with my German classmates that the country still has far to go.

No country is perfect. Every country I can think of has done something regrettable. We should be honest about criticizing other countries, as well as our own. But being prejudiced and making simple generalizations can only make tense international situations worse.

Miranda was 18 when she wrote this story. After high school, she went to Brandeis University.

The Identity Experiment

By Lily Mai

One morning last month, I curled my hair and tied a bit of it back to show my face. I also wore an excessive amount of black eyeliner and dark eye shadow for a "smoky eyes" look. I wore my mother's black shoes with tight blue jeans and a tight black T-shirt to show off my black hair. I thought I looked good and I felt confident.

When I got to school, I saw my good friend in the hallway. She looked at me and said, "I haven't seen you in two weeks and you look good! Wow." I told her I wanted the "dress to kill" look.

She smiled at me, looked me up and down, nodded her head and said, "Yeah, you're definitely dressed to kill."

Every time I went to the bathroom to check my eye makeup, I couldn't help but think about my freshman year and how I never would've done something like this. Back then, I always wore plain clothing. I had fuzzy hair in a ponytail and I didn't use gel or hair spray to make it less puffy. I looked like the stereotypical smart, quiet Chinese girl.

Recently I've started changing—tweezing my eyebrows, styling my hair. But I don't usually wear makeup or shoes with heels, and I was surprised at how much people noticed the change. Later that day, a guy in the hallway looked me in the face and said, "Hey, how you doing, Miss?" I was surprised because that doesn't often happen to me.

When I walked into class, a classmate looked me up and down with a "What's the occasion?" look. Before I knew it, the whole class was saying things like, "What are you doing after school?" and, "Do you have a date?"

All I'd done was add eye makeup and some tight jeans, and people saw me completely differently.

I just blushed and looked away. I didn't want to be the center of the attention. I knew I looked good, but to me it wasn't something to talk or brag about. It was more of an inside kind of feeling for me, a confidence that I'd longed to feel all through high school.

It was amazing. All I'd done was add eye makeup and some tight jeans, and I felt completely different. And other people saw me completely differently, too.

I wondered, "How much does our appearance affect how people perceive us and how we feel about ourselves?" If I got this big a reaction from a little eye shadow, what if I looked completely different? Would people react differently? Would I feel different? I decided to do an experiment to figure out just how much our appearance can shape how we think of ourselves.

I planned to try out different identities on different days— goth, clubber, hip-hop, and my normal look—to see if people would react differently. I'd take the same route home each day and stop at the same corner deli. The only difference would be my appearance. That way I could be sure that anything I was feeling, and any reactions I got, would be based on how I looked.

Day One: Goth

The next day, I came to the Youth Communication office and a goth writer helped me dress like her. I wore a black lace collar, black Converse sneakers, huge baggy black pants with gold zippers everywhere, a spiked belt and silver chains wrapped around my hips. I also wore three huge necklaces, including a heavy back cross on a chain. I wore a massive amount of black makeup—eyeliner, eye shadow, even black lipstick and nail polish. I drew a black star on the bottom of my left eye to enhance the dark look.

When I looked at myself in the mirror, I saw myself as the same person, just wearing a different outfit. I didn't feel different until I was out in public. As I walked along 34th Street, a middle-aged guy looked at me. After we crossed paths, he turned his head and continued to stare. I knew from his eyes that he wasn't looking at me because I was beautiful, but because I looked different.

More heads turned as I continued down 34th Street, and I could see people giving me this "what-the-hell-was-she-thinking" look. Their stares seemed to say I wasn't like them and I didn't belong in this society. I was starting to hate being dressed like this.

After being stared at and even laughed at on the train home, my stomach felt queasy and I was crying inside. I wanted to get out of this outfit now. I didn't want to look like this anymore. I couldn't handle the stress.

I have friends who are goth and they tell me that people often give them stares and they don't care at all. Their attitude is "screw what everyone thinks—normal people suck."

I think these friends dress goth because it's a reflection of who they are, but I don't fully understand it because I'm not like that. I found that I hated the attention. I also think for me it was a little different because I'm Chinese and people aren't used to seeing a

Chinese girl dressed this way.

That evening, I went to a corner deli near my friend's house in Harlem. I'd gone there the day before in my "girly" heels and tight jeans, and the deli guy had given me a horny, turned-on look. But this time he didn't pay any attention to me. He wasn't even looking at me as I bought my M&Ms. I knew right then that people do treat you differently depending on how you dress.

I was relieved to get home that night. Though I liked the comfort of the black baggy pants, I hated people's mean reactions and that they couldn't just accept my style. This was not an identity I'd try again.

Day Two: Downtown Club Girl

For my next outfit, I went for a "downtown, clubbing in the Village" look. After my miserable goth experience, I was excited to look feminine again. I was ready to walk around in my short skirt and I looked forward to people's reactions.

As I was applying my makeup, I thought about how long it was taking me. And even though I don't normally like the idea of being hit on, I found myself thinking, "Someone has to hit on me—all this hard work has to pay off!" I had no idea what I was in for.

Dressed in a green top, a short gauzy black miniskirt and heeled ankle boots, I felt so naked. More naked than I'd ever felt in my entire life. Walking to the subway was embarrassing and I wanted to walk faster to get away, but I couldn't. Not in these shoes. I felt everyone's eyes on my bare legs. I wished I'd brought a pair of jeans with me to hide my legs.

In the subway station, a teenager said to me, "Hey Sweetie," and I felt his eyes roam all over my body. I actually smiled in my head because he was the first to really say something about my outfit, and I found it flattering.

But when I got out of the train, a grown man in his 30s looked at me from head to toe and said, "Mmmm," like I was food and it looked delicious. As I made my way across the street, a man wearing a huge fur coat and handing out fliers said, "Nice legs." I was starting to wish I'd never walked out of the house like this.

As the day went on, I found that I didn't like the attention after all. I felt like my butt was hanging out of my skirt. I felt like people thought I was a slut or a hooker and I hated looking like one. I got comments from three more guys (all grown men) in one block. A guy in a white van even stopped and waved for me to come over to him.

After a while I put on this sad, long, depressed face so people would leave me alone and not think of me as a slut. I told myself, "I'm returning this skirt tomorrow." When I stopped to buy a soda, a man coming out of the store said, "Look at you looking all sexy." In the store, another man said that I had "this innocent face that burns all." I said thank you because I thought it was a compliment, but after I left I wasn't so sure.

Later, I went into that same corner deli where I'd gone the previous two days. This time, the guy behind the deli counter (who'd looked at me hungrily in my girly outfit and ignored me in my goth outfit) looked at me from head to toe as if disgusted. He gave me a dirty look like I was a prostitute. I couldn't wait to get home and change into a pair of jeans.

What surprised me most about dressing in this outfit was that I liked it, at least at first. I liked that it made me feel—and I hate to admit this—pretty inside because of the compliments I got. But after a while, the looks from people on the street made me feel like I was a tramp.

Day Three: Hip-Hop

For my next outfit, I wore a huge, sleeveless basketball jersey and a flat-brimmed baseball cap to go with it, both of which I borrowed from my boyfriend. The jersey was like a dress on me, but I tucked the bottom into my jeans, and with my puffy black down jacket over it, it wasn't too noticeable.

But I felt miserable because I thought I looked boyish. I hated the hugeness of the shirt. And I hate wearing anything on my head because I wear glasses. The cap kept falling on my glasses, which made my glasses keep falling down my face. But most of all, I felt I looked like a fake, trying to look cool.

When I walked the same streets as I had in all my other outfits, the looks I got weren't surprising. People's eyes clung to my face until I passed them, and girls gave me this weird "who is she trying to be, dressing that way" look.

When I was in the deli, a teenage girl looked at me up and down and breathed in my entire outfit. I could tell she thought I was trying too hard to fit in and that made me feel angry because I would never wear something that's not me just to fit in. Even the deli guy looked at me from head to toe with a smirk on his face.

At the end of the day, there was nothing I liked about my hip-hop outfit. I didn't look or feel pretty. The shirt was too long, the cap was huge on my small head and the entire look was way out of my league. I'd never wear it again.

Day 4: The Real Me

After that experience, it was a relief to dress as my regular self the next day. I wore a plain black T-shirt and jeans, with no makeup or accessories. I liked the simplicity of the outfit. I didn't have to worry about whether my eyeliner was smudged or if my earrings went with my outfit or if my hair looked right. I felt so laid back and relaxed, like this was the real me. The quiet, innocent me.

And not surprisingly, I didn't get any reactions the whole day. No looks or "Hey Sweetie" or muttering. It was as if they didn't see me at all. But I saw the real me in that outfit, and I liked it. I'm just another ordinary-looking girl, and I'm happy with that.

This whole experience has taught me a couple of things. It confirmed my idea that we're judged immediately by what we wear. Our clothes are windows into our identities. When strangers see us, they make assumptions about who we are based on our appearance, and they react accordingly.

I also learned how much my feelings about myself are based on other people's reactions. In the goth outfit, I didn't feel one bit different until I went outside. When people started staring and laughing, it really hurt and made me want to take off the outfit right away.

And when I wore the short skirt, I felt flattered by the compliments I got. I'd never thought I was pretty, but those reactions gave me a little hope that I might not be bad looking after all. At the same time, when people looked at me like I was a slut, I felt naked and uncomfortable.

This experience has confirmed my idea that we're judged immediately by what we wear.

When I look in the mirror, I want to see myself in what I wear, and I want other people to see who I am. This experiment gave me a better idea of who that is. I found that I was afraid to wear outfits like goth and hip-hop, but I was excited about wearing the girly outfits. Maybe that's who I am—maybe I'm more of a girly girl than I'd thought.

I think I never admitted that to myself before because I was ashamed of it. I didn't want to be one of those girls who has to buy the latest trends and cries when she breaks a nail. But I actually like wearing girly clothes and a little makeup, and I like getting compliments (as long as they're from guys my age).

I like feeling comfortable too, though. For now, I'll probably keep my same look and just wear a little eye makeup occasionally, and maybe even a skirt. One that covers my legs though—I've already returned the miniskirt.

Lily was 17 when she wrote this story. After high school, she went to Brooklyn College.

Coloring Outside the Lines

By Desiree Bailey

I didn't think much about race until 7th grade, when I joined the gifted class at my school. For the first time, I was the only black person in my class, and I suddenly felt a lot of pressure. I thought that if I didn't do well, my classmates would think it was because I was black. Race suddenly mattered to me, and I felt completely out of place.

It was the first time I'd realized I was a minority. All my life I'd been around a diverse mix of people. On the island of Trinidad, where I was born, the population is mostly of African and Indian descent with a sprinkling of Chinese, Hispanics mainly from Venezuela, Native people (Caribs, Amerindians, and Arawaks), and whites. It seemed to me that almost everyone there lived side by side.

In Rosedale, Queens—the New York City neighborhood that

I immigrated to when I was 8—almost everyone was black. My elementary school was mostly black, but there were also Indians from the Caribbean. Since my neighbors and classmates in New York were similar to the people I lived around in Trinidad, I still didn't think about race.

At home, race had never been a big issue for my mother. She'd acknowledge racial prejudice, but she never dwelled on it. My father, on the other hand, came to America in the 1970s, when black people were struggling for equality and respect. He read a lot about the plight of blacks around the world, and kept us in endless conversations about it. In our kitchen, we even had a beautiful poster depicting all the great kings and queens of Africa's past.

But the discussions were all theoretical to me. My real-life encounters with racism were rare. My 6th grade class at a middle school in Bayside, Queens had a mix of black, white, Asian, and Hispanic kids. There were only a few black kids, unlike my elementary school, which was probably 99.9% black. But I still felt at ease because there was such a diverse mix.

So when I started 7th grade, being the only black kid in my class caught me by surprise. I couldn't blend in anymore. I was easily recognized as "the black kid," and I was afraid of the attention that I might get.

I felt like I wasn't just representing myself, but all black people. For many of my classmates, I imagined I was the first black person they'd ever had a chance to get to know. I worried for the first time that many people didn't see blacks as individuals, but as a stereotype, a group of people who all acted the same: loud, uneducated, and obnoxious.

I assumed that my classmates had those prejudices, and I couldn't make a fool of myself in front of them. I imagined that one little mistake wouldn't just be mine; it would be the mistake of my race.

The pressure I placed on myself made me hesitant to speak. What if I said the wrong thing? What if words flew tangled and contorted out of my nervous mouth? I became quiet. I became even quieter when the topic of black people came up. When we talked about slavery in social studies class, I wanted to disappear. Although I didn't spot any outward signs of racism, I still felt singled out.

My classmates were so cautious around me. When they described black people, they'd pause to search for the best word to use without being offensive. If they described someone white or Asian, I'd never hear that hesitation. Maybe it's because blacks have always had a sensitive position in America. My classmates' self-censorship made me even more uncomfortable and aware of my differences.

Perhaps my insecurities about my people and myself were fueled by negative images of blacks in the media. In the movies I saw, young black men were almost always criminals, blazing a path of destruction wherever they went.

In popular music videos, I saw women of all shades of brown exploited by their own black men. I felt like my race was a big show, a huge entertainment session aimed to amuse, excite, and instill fear in others.

In my neighborhood, some people reinforced these ideas. It began to bug me that many of the black teenagers I saw on the bus were rude and obnoxious. They'd jump on the bus seats, shout at the top of their lungs and pick fights with each other, bothering innocent people who were minding their own business.

Some women would walk around with barely any clothes on while men hooted at them. Many black people I saw seemed to be on edge and angry, or just looking for fun laced with trouble.

I wasn't like that. Instead of wreaking havoc on the bus, I'd quietly read my book. I wasn't rude or a troublemaker, and I didn't want my people to be seen that way.

It's true there were many other black kids like me. Instead of hanging around the block, they read books like I did. They were smart kids with bright futures. But I didn't meet those kids until high school. In 7th grade, I just wanted to fit in with the white and Asian kids in my class.

So I decided that it was up to me to show my classmates that not all black people were loud and obnoxious. I'd teach them that black people could be successful and not like the negative characters that they saw on TV. I'd show them that we could enjoy different types of music and be as open-minded and cultured as anyone else.

In my quest to separate myself from the black stereotypes I thought my classmates expected to see in me, I began to reject things I identified as black. I didn't dare pick up a book by Maya Angelou. I avoided listening to hip-hop and r&b.

Watching popular music videos, I felt like my race was a big show, to amuse, excite, and instill fear in others.

The sounds from my headphones were from bands like Linkin Park, Adema, Staind, and System of a Down. Whatever was rock, I listened to it. At first, I didn't even enjoy the heavier rock. But I wanted to like it, so I listened to it again and again until it became my love. I thought it would help me be more like my classmates. The confusion and swirls of the drums and guitars eventually came to reflect how I felt.

But no matter how hard I blasted my rock music, it didn't help me fit in. My physical differences were clearly pointed out by my classmates. One day, a boy with pale skin and brownish-blond hair asked me about my hair.

"Why is it like that?" he said. He looked at my neatly braided cornrows with a look more of disgust than curiosity. "It's so stiff and it looks like a bunch of train tracks are stuck to your head." I was extremely hurt by his comments. No one had ever been so rude about my race to my face. How could anyone be so obnoxious and unkind?

When I went to the house of another classmate, I felt even more stigmatized. Her mom was Puerto Rican and her dad was

Chinese, and I didn't expect ignorant attitudes from a family with such diversity. But I heard her younger brothers whispering to each other about me.

"Why is she so black?" one said. Another said, "Maybe if she scrubs her skin really hard, it'll come off." They walked into another room laughing while I stood there feeling insulted and uncomfortable. My friend acted as if nothing happened. So did I. I didn't want to make a scene.

Situations like that made me feel even more separated from my peers. I sank deeper and deeper into my rock music. But instead of helping me fit in with the white kids, my music separated me from the few black people I knew in other classes.

One day, I was on the bus going home with two friends, one black and the other Hispanic. One asked what I was listening to, so I gave him my headphones. When he heard the ear-splitting drums of System of a Down and the monstrous growl of the lead singer, he looked at me like I was a joke.

"What the hell is that?" he asked. "Why are you listening to rock? That's white people music." I felt my face grow hot but I didn't know how to respond, so I just laughed his comments off.

All these conflicts upset me. I felt too black for the kids in my class and too white for my friends in other classes. I'd talk and laugh with people, but inside, I just wanted to get away from everyone. Every chance I got, I isolated myself and delved deeper into my books, my writing, and my music. They were my favorite places to escape.

It was hard to for me to realize who I was becoming until I became friends with Jessica in the 8th grade. She was obsessed with insulting her own dark brown skin. She was devastated because she thought she was hideous and wouldn't be loved by anyone.

"I hate myself," she'd say. "I'm so black and ugly." I didn't pay attention to her at first because I thought she was just fishing for compliments. But it didn't take me long to realize that she meant what she said.

She'd look at my friend, Ashley, who was black but light-skinned, and say, "Why can't I be your color?"

Ashley and I worried about her. We told Jessica that skin color and beauty weren't connected, but it was hard to convince her when the media ambushed us with those ideas every day. We couldn't convince her she was wrong about herself, and she eventually withdrew from us.

Seeing how Jessica's negative thoughts destroyed her self-esteem, I began to wonder if I was doing the same thing to myself. When I reexamined my beliefs, I was shocked to realize that all the stereotypes I thought others believed about black people were things I believed.

When I saw black people lazing on street corners, or behaving inappropriately in music videos, I shook my head with disgust. I thought back to all the past struggles and achievements of black people and wondered if my generation would flush it all down the drain.

Instead of looking into situations more deeply, I simply pointed my finger and criticized my people. I realized I was stereotyping my own people as rude and ignorant when I was the one who was rude and ignorant. I had poisoned myself against my race just to fit in with my classmates. I began to think that I was a racist—a racist against my own people.

In my quest to separate myself from the stereotypes, I began to reject things I identified as black.

I decided I couldn't let my fears decide my behavior or tastes anymore. I began to work hard to see people as individuals with interesting lives, instead of simplistic stereotypes.

It's taken several years to change my thinking. At times I still feel extremely different from other people, but now I see it as a good thing. My differences showed me the way to writing, playing the flute and guitar, and my interest in anthropology.

I still have to deal with ignorance about black people from

my white and Asian classmates, and ignorance from black people about my interests. Despite this, I'm committed to being myself instead of trying to represent an entire race. And I'm not going to judge my own race, or any other race, based on stereotypes.

Now I'm in 11th grade and I'm on great terms with myself as a black teenager. It doesn't bother me anymore if I'm seen as "too white" by some and "too black" by others. I know it's impossible to expect everyone to see the world exactly as I do.

My music collection has Alicia Keys and Kanye West next to Coldplay and Jimi Hendrix. Books by Maya Angelou, J.K. Rowling, and Pablo Neruda spill off my shelves.

My music, my literature, and my perspective don't belong to a particular race. They don't have a specific color. They're just what I love.

Desiree was 17 when she wrote this story. After high school, she attended Georgetown University.

FICTION SPECIAL

Lost and Found

Darcy Wills winced at the loud rap music coming from her sister's room.

    My rhymes were rockin'
    MC's were droppin'
    People shoutin' and hip-hoppin'
    Step to me and you'll be inferior
    'Cause I'm your lyrical superior.

Darcy went to Grandma's room. The darkened room smelled of lilac perfume, Grandma's favorite, but since her stroke Grandma did not notice it, or much of anything.

"Bye, Grandma," Darcy whispered from the doorway. "I'm going to school now."

Just then, the music from Jamee's room cut off, and Jamee rushed into the hallway.

The teen characters in the Bluford novels, a fiction series by Townsend Press, struggle with many of the same difficult issues that our students write about. Here's the first chapter from *Lost and Found*, by Anne Schraff, the first book in the series. In this novel, high school sophomore Darcy contends with the return of her long-absent father, the troubling behavior of her younger sister Jamee, and the beginning of her first relationship.

"Like she even hears you," Jamee said as she passed Darcy. Just two years younger than Darcy, Jamee was in eighth grade, though she looked older.

"It's still nice to talk to her. Sometimes she understands. You want to pretend she's not here or something?"

"She's not," Jamee said, grabbing her backpack.

"Did you study for your math test?" Darcy asked. Mom was an emergency room nurse who worked rotating shifts. Most of the time, Mom was too tired to pay much attention to the girls' schoolwork. So Darcy tried to keep track of Jamee.

"Mind your own business," Jamee snapped.

"You got two D's on your last report card," Darcy scolded. "You wanna flunk?" Darcy did not want to sound like a nagging parent, but Jamee wasn't doing her best. Maybe she couldn't make A's like Darcy, but she could do better.

Jamee stomped out of the apartment, slamming the door behind her. "Mom's trying to get some rest!" Darcy yelled. "Do you have to be so selfish?" But Jamee was already gone, and the apartment was suddenly quiet.

Darcy loved her sister. Once, they had been good friends. But now all Jamee cared about was her new group of rowdy friends. They leaned on cars outside of school and turned up rap music on their boom boxes until the street seemed to tremble like an earthquake. Jamee had even stopped hanging out with her old friend Alisha Wrobel, something she used to do every weekend.

Darcy went back into the living room, where her mother sat in the recliner sipping coffee. "I'll be home at 2:30, Mom," Darcy said. Mom smiled faintly. She was tired, always tired. And lately she was worried too. The hospital where she worked was cutting staff. It seemed each day fewer people were expected to do more work. It was like trying to climb a mountain that keeps getting taller as you go. Mom was forty-four, but just yesterday she said, "I'm like an old car that's run out of warranty, baby. You know what happens then. Old car is ready for the junk heap. Well, maybe that hospital is gonna tell me one of these days—'Mattie Mae Wills, we don't need you anymore. We can get somebody younger and cheaper.'"

"Mom, you're not old at all," Darcy had said, but they were only words, empty words. They could not erase the dark, weary lines from beneath her mother's eyes.

Darcy headed down the street toward Bluford High School. It was not a terrible neighborhood they lived in; it just was not good. Many front yards were not cared for. Debris—fast food wrappers, plastic bags, old newspapers—blew around and piled against fences and curbs. Darcy hated that. Sometimes she and other kids from school spent Saturday mornings cleaning up, but it seemed a losing battle. Now, as she walked, she tried to focus on small spots of beauty along the way. Mrs. Walker's pink and white roses bobbed proudly in the morning breeze. The Hustons' rock garden was carefully designed around a wooden windmill.

As she neared Bluford, Darcy thought about the science project that her biology teacher, Ms. Reed, was assigning. Darcy was doing hers on tidal pools. She was looking forward to visiting a real tidal pool, taking pictures, and doing research. Today, Ms. Reed would be dividing the students into teams of two. Darcy wanted to be paired with her close friend, Brisana Meeks. They were both excellent students, a cut above most kids at Bluford, Darcy thought.

"Today, we are forming project teams so that each student can gain something valuable from the other," Ms. Reed said as Darcy sat at her desk. Ms. Reed was a tall, stately woman who reminded Darcy of the Statue of Liberty. She would have been a perfect model for the statue if Lady Liberty had been a black woman. She never would have been called pretty, but it was possible she might have been called a handsome woman. "For this assignment, each of you will be working with someone you've never worked with before."

Darcy was worried. If she was not teamed with Brisana,

maybe she would be teamed with some really dumb student who would pull her down. Darcy was a little ashamed of herself for thinking that way. Grandma used to say that all flowers are equal, but different. The simple daisy was just as lovely as the prize rose. But still Darcy did not want to be paired with some weak partner who would lower her grade.

"Darcy Wills will be teamed with Tarah Carson," Ms. Reed announced.

Darcy gasped. Not Tarah! Not that big, chunky girl with the brassy voice who squeezed herself into tight skirts and wore lime green or hot pink satin tops and cheap jewelry. Not Tarah who hung out with Cooper Hodden, that loser who was barely hanging on to his football eligibility. Darcy had heard that Cooper had been left back once or twice and even got his driver's license as a sophomore. Darcy's face felt hot with anger. Why was Ms. Reed doing this?

Hakeem Randall, a handsome, shy boy who sat in the back row, was teamed with the class blabbermouth, LaShawn Appleby. Darcy had a secret crush on Hakeem since freshman year. So far she had only shared this with her diary, never with another living soul.

It was almost as though Ms. Reed was playing some devilish game. Darcy glanced at Tarah, who was smiling broadly. Tarah had an enormous smile, and her teeth contrasted harshly with her dark red lipstick. "Great," Darcy muttered under her breath.

Ms. Reed ordered the teams to meet so they could begin to plan their projects.

As she sat down by Tarah, Darcy was instantly sickened by a syrupy-sweet odor.

She must have doused herself with cheap perfume this morning, Darcy thought.

"Hey, girl," Tarah said. "Well, don't you look down in the mouth. What's got you lookin' that way?"

It was hard for Darcy to meet new people, especially someone like Tarah, a person Aunt Charlotte would call "low class." These were people who were loud and rude. They drank too much, used drugs, got into fights and ruined the neighborhood. They yelled ugly insults at people, even at their friends. Darcy did not actually know that Tarah did anything like this personally, but she seemed like the type who did.

"I just didn't think you'd be interested in tidal pools," Darcy explained.

Tarah slammed her big hand on the desk, making her gold bracelets jangle like ice cubes in a glass, and laughed. Darcy had never heard a mule bray, but she was sure it made exactly the same sound. Then Tarah leaned close and whispered, "Girl, I don't know a tidal pool from a fool. Ms. Reed stuck us together to mess with our heads, you hear what I'm sayin'?"

"Maybe we could switch to other partners," Darcy said nervously.

A big smile spread slowly over Tarah's face. "Nah, I think I'm gonna enjoy this. You're always sittin' here like a princess collecting your A's. Now you gotta work with a regular person, so you better loosen up, girl!"

Darcy felt as if her teeth were glued to her tongue. She fumbled in her bag for her outline of the project. It all seemed like a horrible joke now. She and Tarah Carson standing knee-deep in the muck of a tidal pool!

"Worms live there, don't they?" Tarah asked, twisting a big gold ring on her chubby finger.

"Yeah, I guess," Darcy replied.

"Big green worms," Tarah continued. "So if you get your feet stuck in the bottom of that old tidal pool, and you can't get out, do the worms crawl up your clothes?"

Darcy ignored the remark. "I'd like for us to go there soon, you know, look around."

"My boyfriend, Cooper, he goes down to the ocean all the time. He can take us. He says he's seen these fiddler crabs. They look like big spiders, and they'll try to bite your toes off. Cooper says so," Tarah said.

"Stop being silly," Darcy shot back. "If you're not even going to be serious . . . "

"You think you're better than me, don't you?" Tarah suddenly growled.

"I never said—" Darcy blurted.

"You don't have to say it, girl. It's in your eyes. You think I'm a low-life and you're something special. Well, I got more friends than you got fingers and toes together. You got no friends, and everybody laughs at you behind your back. Know what the word on you is? Darcy Wills give you the chills."

Just then, the bell rang, and Darcy was glad for the excuse to turn away from Tarah, to hide the hot tears welling in her eyes. She quickly rushed from the classroom, relieved that school was over. Darcy did not think she could bear to sit through another class just now.

Darcy headed down the long street towards home. She did not like Tarah. Maybe it was wrong, but it was true. Still, Tarah's brutal words hurt. Even stupid, awful people might tell you the truth about yourself. And Darcy did not have any real friends, except for Brisana. Maybe the other kids were mocking her behind her back. Darcy was very slender, not as shapely as many of the other girls. She remembered the time when Cooper Hodden was hanging in front of the deli with his friends, and he yelled as Darcy went by, "Hey, is that really a female there? Sure don't look like it. Looks more like an old broomstick with hair." His companions laughed rudely, and Darcy had walked a little faster.

A terrible thought clawed at Darcy. Maybe she was the loser, not Tarah. Tarah was always hanging with a bunch of kids, laughing and joking. She would go down the hall to the lockers and greetings would come from everywhere. "Hey, Tarah!" "What's up, Tar?" "See ya at lunch, girl." When Darcy went to the lockers, there was dead silence.

Darcy usually glanced into stores on her way home from school. She enjoyed looking at the trays of chicken feet and pork ears at the little Asian grocery store. Sometimes she would even steal a glance at the diners sitting by the picture window at the Golden Grill Restaurant. But today she stared straight ahead, her shoulders drooping.

If this had happened last year, she would have gone directly to Grandma's house, a block from where Darcy lived. How many times had Darcy and Jamee run to Grandma's, eaten applesauce cookies, drunk cider, and poured out their troubles to Grandma. Somehow, their problems would always dissolve in the warmth of her love and wisdom. But now Grandma was a frail figure in the corner of their apartment, saying little. And what little she did say made less and less sense.

Darcy was usually the first one home. The minute she got there, Mom left for the hospital to take the 3:00 to 11:00 shift in the ER. By the time Mom finished her paperwork at the hospital, she would be lucky to be home again by midnight. After Mom left, Darcy went to Grandma's room to give her the malted nutrition drink that the doctor ordered her to have three times a day.

"Want to drink your chocolate malt, Grandma?" Darcy asked, pulling up a chair beside Grandma's bed.

Grandma was sitting up, and her eyes were open. "No. I'm not hungry," she said listlessly. She always said that.

"You need to drink your malt, Grandma," Darcy insisted, gently putting the straw between the pinched lips.

Grandma sucked the malt slowly. "Grandma, nobody likes me at school," Darcy said. She did not expect any response. But there was a strange comfort in telling Grandma anyway. "Everybody laughs at me. It's because I'm shy and maybe stuck-up, too, I guess. But I don't mean to be. Stuck-up, I mean. Maybe I'm weird. I could be weird, I guess. I could be like Aunt Charlotte . . ." Tears rolled down Darcy's cheeks. Her heart ached with loneliness. There was nobody to talk to anymore, nobody who had time to listen, nobody who understood.

Grandma blinked and pushed the straw away. Her eyes brightened as they did now and then. "You are a wonderful girl. Everybody knows that," Grandma said in an almost normal voice. It happened like that sometimes. It was like being in the middle of a dark storm and having the clouds part, revealing a patch of clear, sunlit blue. For just a few precious minutes, Grandma was bright-eyed and saying normal things.

"Oh, Grandma, I'm so lonely," Darcy cried, pressing her head against Grandma's small shoulder.

"You were such a beautiful baby," Grandma said, stroking her hair." 'That one is going to shine like the morning star.' That's what I told your Mama. 'That child is going to shine like the morning star.' Tell me, Angelcake, is your daddy home yet?"

Darcy straightened. "Not yet." Her heart pounded so hard, she could feel it thumping in her chest. Darcy's father had not been home in five years.

"Well, tell him to see me when he gets home. I want him to buy you that blue dress you liked in the store window. That's for you, Angelcake. Tell him I've got money. My social security came, you know. I have money for the blue dress," Grandma said, her eyes slipping shut.

Just then, Darcy heard the apartment door slam. Jamee had come home. Now she stood in the hall, her hands belligerently on her hips. "Are you talking to Grandma again?" Jamee demanded.

"She was talking like normal," Darcy said. "Sometimes she does. You know she does."

"That is so stupid," Jamee snapped. "She never says anything right anymore. Not anything!" Jamee's voice trembled.

Darcy got up quickly and set down the can of malted milk. She ran to Jamee and put her arms around her sister. "Jamee, I know you're hurting too."

"Oh, don't be stupid," Jamee protested, but Darcy hugged her more tightly, and in a few seconds Jamee was crying. "She was the best thing in this stupid house," Jamee cried. "Why'd she have to go?"

"She didn't go," Darcy said. "Not really."

"She did! She did!" Jamee sobbed. She struggled free of Darcy, ran to her room, and slammed the door. In a minute, Darcy heard the bone-rattling sound of rap music.

Lost and Found, a Bluford Series™ novel, is reprinted with permission from Townsend Press. Copyright © 2002.

Want to read more? This and other Bluford Series™ novels and paperbacks can be purchased for $1 each at www.townsendpress.com.

Teens:
How to Get More Out of This Book

Self-help: The teens who wrote the stories in this book did so because they hope that telling their stories will help readers who are facing similar challenges. They want you to know that you are not alone, and that taking specific steps can help you manage or overcome very difficult situations. They've done their best to be clear about the actions that worked for them so you can see if they'll work for you.

Writing: You can also use the book to improve your writing skills. Each teen in this book wrote 5-10 drafts of his or her story before it was published. If you read the stories closely you'll see that the teens work to include a beginning, a middle, and an end, and good scenes, description, dialogue, and anecdotes (little stories). To improve your writing, take a look at how these writers construct their stories. Try some of their techniques in your own writing.

Reading: Finally, you'll notice that we include the first chapter from a Bluford Series novel in this book, alongside the true stories by teens. We hope you'll like it enough to continue reading. The more you read, the more you'll strengthen your reading skills. Teens at Youth Communication like the Bluford novels because they explore themes similar to those in their own stories. Your school may already have the Bluford books. If not, you can order them online for only $1.

Resources on the Web

We will occasionally post Think About It questions on our website, www.youthcomm.org, to accompany stories in this and other Youth Communication books. We try out the questions with teens and post the ones they like best. Many teens report that writing answers to those questions in a journal is very helpful.

How to Use This Book in Staff Training

Staff say that reading these stories gives them greater insight into what teens are thinking and feeling, and new strategies for working with them. You can help the staff you work with by using these stories as case studies.

Select one story to read in the group, and ask staff to identify and discuss the main issue facing the teen. There may be disagreement about this, based on the background and experience of staff. That is fine. One point of the exercise is that teens have complex lives and needs. Adults can probably be more effective if they don't focus too narrowly and can see several dimensions of their clients.

Ask staff: What issues or feelings does the story provoke in them? What kind of help do they think the teen wants? What interventions are likely to be most promising? Least effective? Why? How would you build trust with the teen writer? How have other adults failed the teen, and how might that affect his or her willingness to accept help? What other resources would be helpful to this teen, such as peer support, a mentor, counseling, family therapy, etc?

Resources on the Web

From time to time we will post Think About It questions on our website, www.youthcomm.org, to accompany stories in this and other Youth Communication books. We try out the questions with teens and post the ones that they find most effective. We'll also post lessons for some of the stories. Adults can use the questions and lessons in workshops.

> **Discussion Guide**

Teachers and Staff:
How to Use This Book in Groups

When working with teens individually or in groups, you can use these stories to help young people face difficult issues in a way that feels safe to them. That's because talking about the issues in the stories usually feels safer to teens than talking about those same issues in their own lives. Addressing issues through the stories allows for some personal distance; they hit close to home, but not too close. Talking about them opens up a safe place for reflection. As teens gain confidence talking about the issues in the stories, they usually become more comfortable talking about those issues in their own lives.

Below are general questions to guide your discussion. In most cases you can read a story and conduct a discussion in one 45-minute session. Teens are usually happy to read the stories aloud, with each teen reading a paragraph or two. (Allow teens to pass if they don't want to read.) It takes 10-15 minutes to read a story straight through. However, it is often more effective to let workshop participants make comments and discuss the story as you go along. The workshop leader may even want to annotate her copy of the story beforehand with key questions.

If teens read the story ahead of time or silently, it's good to break the ice with a few questions that get everyone on the same page: Who is the main character? How old is she? What happened to her? How did she respond? Another good starting question is: "What stood out for you in the story?" Go around the room and let each person briefly mention one thing.

Then move on to open-ended questions, which encourage participants to think more deeply about what the writers were feeling, the choices they faced, and the actions they took. There are no right or wrong answers to the open-ended questions.

Open-ended questions encourage participants to think about how the themes, emotions, and choices in the stories relate to their own lives. Here are some examples of open-ended questions that we have found to be effective. You can use variations of these questions with almost any story in this book.

—What main problem or challenge did the writer face?

—What choices did the teen have in trying to deal with the problem?

—Which way of dealing with the problem was most effective for the teen? Why?

—What strengths, skills, or resources did the teen use to address the challenge?

—If you were in the writer's shoes, what would you have done?

—What could adults have done better to help this young person?

—What have you learned by reading this story that you didn't know before?

—What, if anything, will you do differently after reading this story?

—What surprised you in this story?

—Do you have a different view of this issue, or see a different way of dealing with it, after reading this story? Why or why not?

Credits

The stories in this book originally appeared in the following Youth Communication publications:

"Group Home Child" by Keniel Simpson, *Represent*, March/April 2000; "Princess Oreo Speaks Out" by Dwan Carter, *New Youth Connections*, March 2001; "Out, Without a Doubt" by Xavier Reyes, *Represent*, January/February 1997; "A Different Kind of Friend" by Latoya Souvenir, *New Youth Connections*, September/October 1995; "Stop Following Me" by Stephanie Hinkson, *New Youth Connections*, April 2005; "I'm Not What You Expect Me to Be" by Jordan Yue, *New Youth Connections*, January/February 2004; "How I Overcame a Mugging—And Prejudice" by Kenneth Schlapp, *New Youth Connections*, December 1986; "My Hospital Internship: Learning to Care" by Sheela Pai, *New Youth Connections*, September/October 1994; "My Secret Love" by Anonymous, *New Youth Connections*, September/October 2000; "Getting Ghetto" by Fred Wagenhauser, *Represent*, May/June 2007; "Dream Girl" by Rance Scully, *New Youth Connections*, September/October 1995; "Rappin' With the 5-0" by Allen Francis, *New Youth Connections*, May/June 1997; "At Home in the Projects" by Fabiola Duvalsaint, *New Youth Connections*, November 1997; "Stupid Questions About Africa" by Aissata Kebe, *New Youth Connections*, January/February 2006; "He Was Black, I Was Asian: A Different Type of Friendship" by Priscilla Chan, *New Youth Connections*, May/June 1995; "She's Cool, She's Funny, She's Gay: My Favorite Sister" by Sandra Leon, *New Youth Connections*, June 1992; "A Classmate in a Wheelchair: I Didn't Know How to Act" by Esther Rajavelu, *New Youth Connections*, September/October 1995; "Why No One Knows I'm a Foster Child" by Shaniqua Sockwell, *Represent*, March/April 1994; "Supermarket Stories: The Lowdown on Aisle Seven" by Tony Cedor, *New Youth Connections*, June 1992; "They Called Me Ch-nk: Unwelcome in the Hood" by George Yi, *New Youth Connections*, December 1995; "Long-Distance Patriot" by Miranda Neubauer, *New Youth Connections*, November 2004; "The Identity Experiment" by Lily Mai, *New Youth Connections*, March 2006; "Coloring Outside the Lines" by Desiree Bailey, *New Youth Connections*, March 2006.

About Youth Communication

Youth Communication, founded in 1980, is a nonprofit youth development program located in New York City whose mission is to teach writing, journalism, and leadership skills. The teenagers we train become writers for our websites and books and for two print magazines: *New Youth Connections*, a general-interest youth magazine, and *Represent*, a magazine by and for young people in foster care.

Each year, up to 100 young people participate in Youth Communication's school-year and summer journalism workshops, where they work under the direction of full-time professional editors. Most are African-American, Latino, or Asian, and many are recent immigrants. The opportunity to reach their peers with accurate portrayals of their lives and important self-help information motivates the young writers to create powerful stories.

Our goal is to run a strong youth development program in which teens produce high quality stories that inform and inspire their peers. Doing so requires us to be sensitive to the complicated lives and emotions of the teen participants while also providing an intellectually rigorous experience. We achieve that goal in the writing/teaching/editing relationship, which is the core of our program.

Our teaching and editorial process begins with discussions

between adult editors and the teen staff. In those meetings, the teens and the editors work together to identify the most important issues in the teens' lives and to figure out how those issues can be turned into stories that will resonate with teen readers.

Once story topics are chosen, students begin the process of crafting their stories. For a personal story, that means revisiting events in one's past to understand their significance for the future. For a commentary, it means developing a logical and persuasive point of view. For a reported story, it means gathering information through research and interviews. Students look inward and outward as they try to make sense of their experiences and the world around them and find the points of intersection between personal and social concerns. That process can take a few weeks or a few months. Stories frequently go through ten or more drafts as students work under the guidance of their editors, the way any professional writer does.

Many of the students who walk through our doors have uneven skills, as a result of poor education, living under extremely stressful conditions, or coming from homes where English is a second language. Yet, to complete their stories, students must successfully perform a wide range of activities, including writing and rewriting, reading, discussion, reflection, research, interviewing, and typing. They must work as members of a team and they must accept individual responsibility. They learn to provide constructive criticism, and to accept it. They engage in explorations of truthfulness, fairness, and accuracy. They meet deadlines. They must develop the audacity to believe that they have something important to say and the humility to recognize that saying it well is not a process of instant gratification. Rather, it usually requires a long, hard struggle through many discussions and much rewriting.

It would be impossible to teach these skills and dispositions as separate, disconnected topics, like grammar, ethics, or assertiveness. However, we find that students make rapid progress when they are learning skills in the context of an inquiry that is personally significant to them and that will benefit their peers.

When teens publish their stories—in *New Youth Connections* and *Represent*, on the web, and in other publications—they reach tens of thousands of teen and adult readers. Teachers, counselors, social workers, and other adults circulate the stories to young people in their classes and out-of-school youth programs. Adults tell us that teens in their programs—including many who are ordinarily resistant to reading—clamor for the stories. Teen readers report that the stories give them information they can't get anywhere else, and inspire them to reflect on their lives and open lines of communication with adults.

Writers usually participate in our program for one semester, though some stay much longer. Years later, many of them report that working here was a turning point in their lives—that it helped them acquire the confidence and skills that they needed for success in college and careers. Scores of our graduates have overcome tremendous obstacles to become journalists, writers, and novelists. They include National Book Award finalist and MacArthur Fellowship winner Edwidge Danticat, novelist Ernesto Quiñonez, writer Veronica Chambers, and *New York Times* reporter Rachel Swarns. Hundreds more are working in law, business, and other careers. Many are teachers, principals, and youth workers, and several have started nonprofit youth programs themselves and work as mentors—helping another generation of young people develop their skills and find their voices.

Youth Communication is a nonprofit educational corporation. Contributions are gratefully accepted and are tax deductible to the fullest extent of the law.

To make a contribution, or for information about our publications and programs, including our catalog of over 100 books and curricula for hard-to-reach teens, see www.youthcomm.org

About the Editors

Virginia Vitzthum is an editor at *Represent*, Youth Communication's magazine by and for teens in foster care. Before working at Youth Communication she wrote a book about Internet dating and a column for the web magazine salon.com. She's also written for *Ms.*, *Elle*, *the Village Voice*, *Time Out New York*, *Washington City Paper*, and other publications. She has edited law books as well as books about substance abuse treatment and health care policy newsletters. She's written a play and a screenplay; produced several short videos; and volunteered at the 52nd St. Project, a children's theater, where she helped 9- to 11-year-olds write plays.

Keith Hefner co-founded Youth Communication in 1980 and has directed it ever since. He is the recipient of the Luther P. Jackson Education Award from the New York Association of Black Journalists and a MacArthur Fellowship. He was also a Revson Fellow at Columbia University.

Laura Longhine is the editorial director at Youth Communication. She edited *Represent*, Youth Communication's magazine by and for youth in foster care, for three years, and has written for a variety of publications. She has a BA in English from Tufts University and an MS in Journalism from Columbia University.

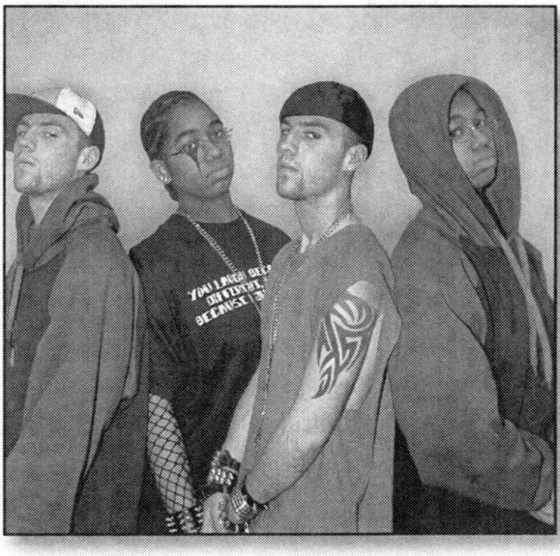

More Helpful Books From Youth Communication

The Struggle to Be Strong: True Stories by Teens About Overcoming Tough Times. Foreword by Veronica Chambers. Help young people identify and build on their own strengths with 30 personal stories about resiliency. (Free Spirit)

Starting With "I": Personal Stories by Teenagers. "Who am I and who do I want to become?" Thirty-five stories examine this question through the lens of race, ethnicity, gender, sexuality, family, and more. Increase this book's value with the free Teacher's Guide, available from youthcomm.org. (Youth Communication)

Real Stories, Real Teens. Inspire teens to read and recognize their strengths with this collection of 26 true stories by teens. The young writers describe how they overcame significant challenges and stayed true to themselves. Also includes the first chapters from three novels in the Bluford Series. (Youth Communication)

The Courage to Be Yourself: True Stories by Teens About Cliques, Conflicts, and Overcoming Peer Pressure. In 26 first-person stories, teens write about their lives with searing honesty. These stories will inspire young readers to reflect on their own lives, work through their problems, and help them discover who they really are. (Free Spirit)

Out With It: Gay and Straight Teens Write About Homosexuality. Break stereotypes and provide support with this unflinching look at gay life from a teen's perspective. With a focus on urban youth, this book also includes several heterosexual teens' transformative experiences with gay peers. (Youth Communication)

Things Get Hectic: Teens Write About the Violence That Surrounds Them. Violence is commonplace in many teens' lives, be it bullying, gangs, dating, or family relationships. Hear the experiences of victims, perpetrators, and witnesses through more than 50 real-world stories. (Youth Communication)

From Dropout to Achiever: Teens Write About School. Help teens overcome the challenges of graduating, which may involve overcoming family problems, bouncing back from a bad semester, or even dropping out for a time. These teens show how they achieve academic success. (Youth Communication)

My Secret Addiction: Teens Write About Cutting. These true accounts of cutting, or self-mutilation, offer a window into the personal and family situations that lead to this secret habit, and show how teens can get the help they need. (Youth Communication)

Sticks and Stones: Teens Write About Bullying. Shed light on bullying, as told from the perspectives of the bully, the victim, and the witness. These stories show why bullying occurs, the harm it causes, and how it might be prevented. (Youth Communication)

Boys to Men: Teens Write About Becoming a Man. The young men in this book write about confronting the challenges of growing up. Their honesty and courage make them role models for teens who are bombarded with contradictory messages about what it means to be a man. (Youth Communication)

Through Thick and Thin: Teens Write About Obesity, Eating Disorders, and Self Image. Help teens who struggle with obesity, eating disorders, and body weight issues. These stories show the pressures teens face when they are confronted by unrealistic standards for physical appearance, and how emotions can affect the way we eat. (Youth Communication)

To order these and other books, go to:
www.youthcomm.org
or call 212-279-0708 x115